COUNTRY CRAFTS
& COOKING

COUNTRY CRAFTS & COOKING

Inspirational ideas for natural gifts, decorations and recipes

TESSA EVELEGH, KATHERINE RICHMOND, AND LIZ TRIGG

PHOTOGRAPHS BY

MICHELLE GARRETT

LORENZ BOOKS

LONDON • NEW YORK • SYDNEY • BATH

First published by Lorenz Books in 1997

© 1997 Anness Publishing Limited

Lorenz Books is an imprint of
Anness Publishing Limited
Hermes House
88–89 Blackfriars Road
London SE1 8HA

A CIP catalogue record for this book is available from the British Library.

ISBN 1 85967 603 0

Publisher: Joanna Lorenz
Project Editor: Christopher Fagg
Editor: Lydia Darbyshire
Designer: Siân Keogh
Photographers: Michelle Garrett, Lucy Mason, Gloria Nicol

Printed and bound in Singapore

This book was previously published as part of a larger compendium, *Country*.

Contributors: Fiona Barnett, Tessa Evelegh, Caroline Kelly, Katherine Richmond, Zoe Smith,
Isabel Stanley, Liz Trigg, Jenny Watson, Dorothy Wood

For all recipes, quantities are given in both metric and imperial measures and, where appropriate,
measures are also given in standard cups and spoons. Follow one set, but not a mixture, because
they are not interchangeable. Size 3 (standard) eggs should be used unless otherwise stated.

1 3 5 7 9 10 8 6 4 2

Contents

INTRODUCTION 6

Country Crafts

TOKENS TO TREASURE 10

Country Cooking

SPRING RECIPES 84

SUMMER RECIPES 102

AUTUMN RECIPES 122

WINTER RECIPES 142

INDEX 158

ACKNOWLEDGEMENTS 160

Introduction

Everyone dreams of an idealized world where the pressures of modern life slip away, days are full of sunshine, vegetables are harvested fresh from the garden, fruit hangs from bushes and trees, an old fruit press squeezes out fresh apple juice in the barn and the house is full of flowers, the scent of thyme and lavender and the heady smell of freshly baking bread. It may not be possible to realize this dream; not everyone wants to live that close to nature, but many people would like to bring a small part of country peace and tranquillity into the pressurized existence of the late twentieth century.

One way this can be achieved is through the recreation of country crafts and using country recipes in the kitchen. This has a twofold benefit. The practice of country crafts produces an atmosphere of calm and truth within the household: making lavender bags, for instance, which scent clothes and deter moths so beautifully, is both practical and useful, but it also means that less attention is paid to the gods of twentieth-century living – the television and radio – and in a small way, it increases the spirituality of life.

Country Crafts and Cooking sets out a number of the traditional country craft projects that can be practised in every home, be it in the depths of the country or in the heart of the city. Concentrating on traditional herbal recipes and remedies taken from old country folklore, the first part of the book outlines many ideas that are both practical and therapeutic. Among the easiest are the old-fashioned pomanders, so useful for scenting rooms and clothes, and there are also cleansing lotions, hair tonic and aftershave, herbal pots and sleep pillows and many other country-style gifts suitable for Christmas, Easter and Thanksgiving. These country tokens all have a practical use and can be created by anyone who wishes to bring a touch of country to their home.

All the projects call for traditional country ingredients that can nowadays be gathered in the garden or readily bought in local markets. They are all simple and satisfying.

Country cooking goes hand in hand with country crafts. Country cooking is a state of mind, a determination not to succumb to the prepackaged, prefabricated ready meals so easily available in supermarkets and stores but to produce food that really tastes like food, that tastes of the country and that uses fresh ingredients in season at the right time of the year.

This is simpler if you have a vegetable garden where you can grow your own fruit and vegetables, but it can be practised by any cook who is determined enough to search out the best and freshest ingredients in markets and to use only those when preparing food for the family.

The mouth-watering recipes in *Country Crafts and Cooking* are divided into the four seasons of the year, which determine the rhythm of country living. In the spring come the first fresh, young, tasty vegetables, spring chicken and lamb and dishes embellished with fresh leeks and onions. The summer brings mint and herbs, used to make fresh mint ice cream, the first strawberries of the year, delicious new potatoes dug straight from the earth and tender young beans and asparagus, while autumn is also a time of plenty. There are apples on the trees and blackberries in the hedges, mushrooms in the fields and a cornucopia of vegetables to be harvested. In the winter as the nights draw in and the family gathers around the fire, the country cook concentrates on traditional stews, thick, warming lentil soups, and the festive Christmas puddings and shortbread.

The country year is seen more clearly in the kitchen than anywhere else in the house, and the recipes in *Country Crafts and Cooking* will provide a rich source of inspiration to help you create a warm, welcoming atmosphere. So follow your instincts and enjoy the charm of country life.

COUNTRY
Crafts

Tokens to Treasure

....

*What can bring more pleasure than gifts inspired by
country traditions? They have a quality that
acknowledges the seasons and withstands the test of
time. Gather together all the natural materials
you can find – shells, papers, natural fabrics, wire,
and even chicken-wire – and turn them into
something very special.*

Sleep Pillow

Many people still swear by sleep pillows, which are traditionally filled with chamomile and hops. Since hops are related to the cannabis plant, they induce a feeling of sleepy well-being, while chamomile helps you to relax. Either buy ready-prepared sleep mix, or make up your own with chamomile, lemon verbena and a few hops. Stitch a pillow filled with these relaxing herbs to keep on your bed, and look forward to some good night's sleep.

MATERIALS

linen muslin, 2 m × 20 cm / 80 × 8 in (this can be made up of two or more shorter lengths)
pins, needle and thread
scissors
pure cotton fabric, 50 × 25 cm / 20 × 10 in
herbal sleep mix
1 m / 39 in antique lace
1 m / 39 in ribbon, 1 cm / ½ in wide
4 pearl buttons

1

Prepare the linen muslin border by stitching together enough lengths to make up 2 m / 80 in. With right sides facing, stitch the ends together to form a ring. Trim the seam. Fold the ring in half lengthways with wrong sides facing and run a line of gathering stitches close to the raw edges.

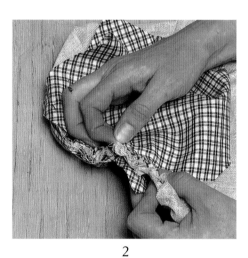

2

Cut two pieces of cotton fabric into 25 cm / 10 in squares. Pull up the gathering threads of the muslin to fit the cushion edge. Pin it to the right side of one square, with raw edges facing outwards, matching the raw edges and easing the gathers evenly round the cushion. Put the second square on top and pin the corners. Stitch the seams, leaving a gap for stuffing. Trim the seams.

3

Turn the cushion right-side out and fill it with herbal sleep mix. Stitch the gap to enclose the border.

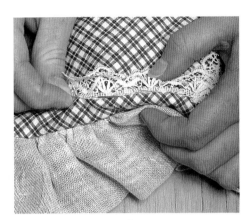

4

Using tiny stitches, sew the lace to the
cushion about 2.5 cm / 1 in away
from the border.

5

Stitch the ribbon close to the lace, making
a neat diagonal fold at the corners.

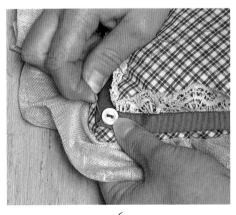

6

Finish by sewing a tiny pearl button
to each corner.

Herb Pot-mat

Protect tabletops from hot pots and pans with an aromatic mat, filled with cinnamon, cloves and bay leaves. The heat of the pot immediately releases the piquancy of its contents, kept evenly distributed with mattress-style ties.

MATERIALS

scissors
ticking, at least 62 × 55 cm /
25 × 22 in
pins, needle and thread

spice mix to fill, e.g. dried bay
leaves, cloves, cinnamon sticks
heavy-duty upholstery needle
cotton string

1

First make the hanger by cutting a strip of ticking 5 × 30 cm / 2 × 12 in. With right sides facing, fold this in half lengthways. Stitch the long side, leaving the ends open. Trim the seam. Turn right side out and press. Fold in half to form a loop. Cut two rectangles from the fabric measuring about 62 × 50 cm / 25 × 20 in.

2

Place the cushion pieces on a flat surface, right sides facing, and then slip the hanging loop between the layers, with the raw edges pointing out towards a corner.

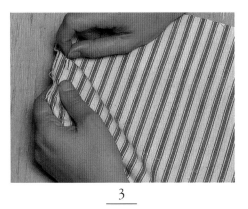

3

Pin and stitch the cushion pieces together, leaving about 7.5 cm / 3 in open. Trim the seams. Turn right side out.

4

Fill the cushion with the spices.

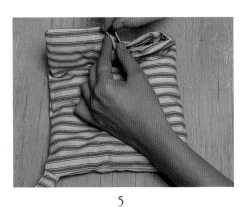

5

Slip-stitch to close the opening.

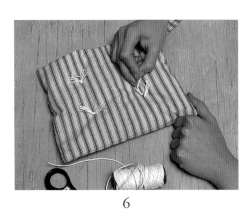

6

Using a heavy-duty upholstery needle threaded with cotton string, make a stitch about a third in from two sides of the cushion, clearing the spices inside the mat away from the area as you go. Untwist the strands of the string for a more feathery look. Repeat with three other ties to give a mattress effect. Make a simple knot in each to secure the ties.

Lavender Sachets

Use fabric scraps to appliqué simple motifs on to charming chequered fabrics, and then stitch them into sachets to fill with lavender and use as drawer-fresheners. Inspired by traditional folk art, these have universal appeal.

MATERIALS
scissors
fabric scraps
paper for templates
pins, needle and thread
stranded embroidery thread in
different colours
loose dried lavender
button

1
Cut two pieces of fabric into squares about 15 cm / 6 in. If you are using a checked or striped fabric, it is a good idea to let the design dictate the exact size. Scale up the template and use it as a pattern to cut bird and wing shapes from contrasting fabrics. Pin and tack the bird shape to the right side of one square.

2
Neatly slip-stitch the bird shape to the sachet front, turning in the edges as you go. Repeat with the wing shape.

3
Using three strands of embroidery thread in a contrasting colour, make neat running stitches around the bird and its wing.

4
Make long stitches on the tail and wing to indicate feathers, graduating them into a pleasing shape. Sew in the button eye.

5
With right sides facing, stitch the front and back of the sachet together, leaving a 5 cm / 2 in gap. Trim the seams. Turn it right-side out and press. Fill with dried lavender, and then slip-stitch to close the gap.

Lacy Lavender Heart

*Evocative of the Victorian era, this exquisitely pretty heart-shaped lavender bag
is made from simple, creamy muslin, and trimmed with antique lace and
satin ribbon. The chiffon ribbon at the top is tied into a loop for hanging on
coat hangers with favourite garments.*

MATERIALS

paper for template *scissors* *silky muslin, about* *60 × 20 cm / 24 × 8 in*	*pins, needle and stranded* *embroidery thread* *pearl button* *loose dried lavender*	*50 cm / 20 in antique lace* *50 cm / 20 in very narrow* *satin ribbon* *50 cm / 20 in medium ribbon*

1

Make a heart-shaped paper template about
15 cm / 6 in high and use this as a pattern.
Cut four heart shapes from muslin. Tack
the hearts together in pairs so each heart is
a double thickness of muslin.

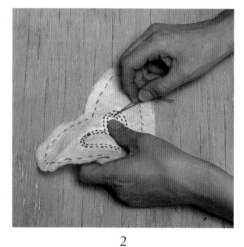

2

Cut a smaller heart shape from muslin.
Carefully stitch this to the centre front of one
of the larger heart shapes, using two strands
of embroidery thread and a running stitch.
Make another row of running stitches
inside this.

3

Sew the button to the top
of the smaller heart.

4

Stitch a third row of running stitches inside
the other two. Allow the edges of the smaller
heart to fray. With right sides facing, stitch
all around the edge of the two large double-
thickness muslin heart shapes, leaving a gap
of 5 cm / 2 in. Trim the seams, snip into
the seam at the 'V' of the heart and snip off
the bottom point within the seam allowance.
Turn the heart right-side out. Fill it with
lavender and slip-stitch to close the gap.
Don't despair if the heart looks pretty
miserable and misshapen at this stage!

5

Carefully slip-stitch the lace around the edge
of the heart.

6

Stitch the satin ribbon over the lower edge
of the lace.

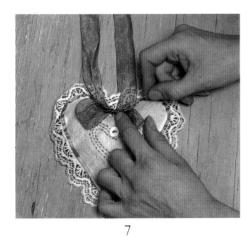

7

Finish with a ribbon bow, arranging it so the
long tails are upwards as these can then be
joined to form a loop for hanging on
coat hangers in the wardrobe.

Lavender Bag

Stars are frequently found in patchwork, and the LeMoyne Star is a popular pattern. To achieve this tricky eight-seam join, which meets in the centre of the star, work slowly and carefully.

MATERIALS

tracing paper and pencil
thin card
craft knife
scraps of silk organza in 3 colours
rotary cutter (optional)
scrap of lining silk
dressmaker's pins
sewing machine and matching thread
needle and matching thread
dried lavender
ribbon

1

Trace the star and make the templates. For each star (you will need 2) cut out 8 pieces from template 1 in 2 colours and 4 pieces each from templates 2 and 3 in the third colour. Use a rotary cutter if you wish.

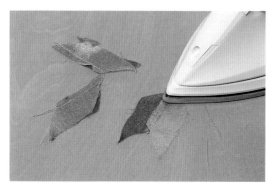

2

To make the star, with right sides facing, pin together 2 piece 1s that are in different colours, and stitch them together. Make another pair to match. Press the seams flat but not open, to reduce bulk.

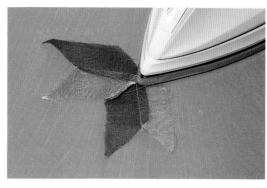

3

Join the 2 pairs together, carefully matching the centre seams, pin and stitch. Press the seams flat. Make the other half of the star in the same way.

4

To set in a square 3, swivel the square to match the corner points and pin to the angled edge. To set in a triangle 2, match the corner points and pin to the angled edge. Stitch and press.

5

Set in 3 more triangles to make the patch. Make a second patch in the same way. Measure one side and cut 2 pieces of organza to this length but 5 cm/2 in wide. Stitch one to the top of each patch and press. Right sides facing, stitch around the base and sides of the bag and turn through. Fold a 1 cm/½ in hem around the top of the bag, press and top stitch. Fill the bag with dried lavender and tie with a ribbon bow.

LeMoyne Star

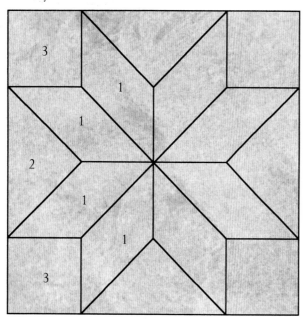

Little House Key Ring

Keep your keys safe on this pretty key ring. The little house is made from tiny patched pieces which are appliquéd on to the fob.

MATERIALS

*tracing paper, paper and pencil
dressmaker's scissors
red and blue gingham and red fabric scraps
needle and tacking thread
iron
cream cotton fabric,
10 × 32 cm / 4 × 13 in
wadding (batting),
10 × 15 cm / 4 × 6 in red,
cream and blue
sewing threads
key ring*

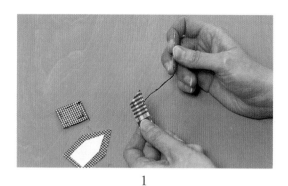

1

Trace the design on to paper and cut out 2 windows, 2 walls, 2 chimneys, a roof and a door. Cut out in scraps of fabric with a 6 mm / ¼ in seam allowance. Tack to the backing papers and press.

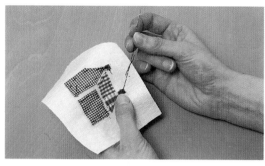

2

Cut 2 main pieces from cream cotton fabric and 2 from wadding (batting). Tack the house in sections to one piece of cotton fabric, removing the paper as you go. Slip stitch the pieces in position with matching thread.

3

Sandwich the wadding between the appliquéd and plain fabrics, and tack through all the layers to secure.

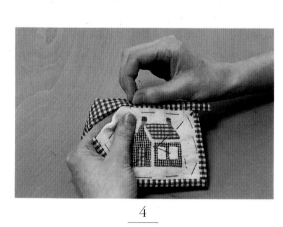

4

Cut 3 bias strips in gingham. Press under 6 mm / ¼ in turnings and bind the raw edges leaving 2.5 cm / 1 in free either side of the point. Thread the ends through the key ring and slip stitch together.

Key fob and motif template

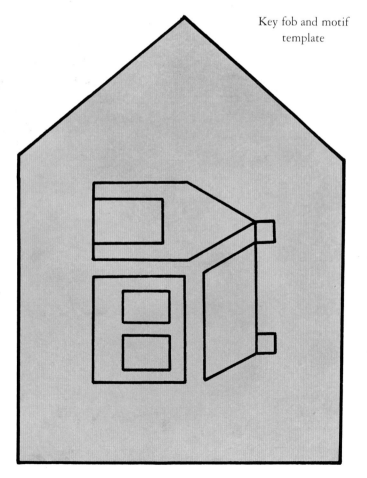

Patchwork Cards

Patchwork designs like this Northumberland star can be used to make unusual gift cards. Work out a design on paper and trace the design on to the bonding web.

MATERIALS

tracing paper and pencil
ruler
iron-on fusible bonding web
iron
assortment of fabric scraps
dressmaker's scissors
coloured card
metallic marker pen

1

Cut out the shapes. Iron the shapes on to the back of the fabric scraps and cut out without a seam allowance.

2

Lay the shapes on the card to make up the design. Cover with a clean cloth and iron. Outline the design with the marker pen.

Photo Frame

Blue and white checked fabrics make a fresh-looking border for a favourite photo.

Cut out a centre square from one piece of the card, leaving a 5 cm / 2 in border. Cut 4 gingham border strips 27 × 10 cm / 11 × 4 in. Cut 4 7 cm / 3 in squares of cream fabric and press under the raw edges to make 5 cm / 2 in squares. Iron bonding web to the reverse of the fabric scraps and cut out 4 flower shapes and 4 pairs of leaves.

MATERIALS

2 pieces of thick card,
22 cm / 8 in square
craft knife
scraps of blue and white
gingham and checked
fabric
dressmaker's scissors
scraps of cream fabric
iron
iron-on fusible bonding
web
assorted scraps of fabric for
the flowers
green and navy embroidery
threads
crewel needle
dressmaker's pins
needle and matching
thread
fabric glue
double-sided tape

1

Pull off the backing from the bonding web and iron a flower and leaves motif to the corner of each cream square, as shown. Embroider the stems in green thread. Cut 4 narrow strips of checked fabric 27 cm / 11 in long and press under the long edges. Pin and stitch along the centre of the gingham borders.

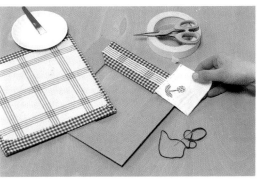

2

Glue the cream squares to the corners of the frame, with the flowers facing outwards. Work large stab stitches round the squares in navy thread. Fold the border fabric to the back of the frame and secure with tape. Cover the other piece of card with fabric, then slip stitch the 2 pieces together round 3 sides, leaving one side open.

Gift Tag

This gift tag would also look very pretty hanging from the wardrobe door key.

MATERIALS

*8 cm / 3 in square of
18-count Rustico, Zweigart
E3292
stranded cotton DMC nos.
500, 550, 552, 554,
3363, 3364 and 3820
tapestry needle
15 cm / 6 in square of
natural handmade paper
craft knife
safety ruler
scissors
all-purpose glue
single hole punch
two reinforcing rings*

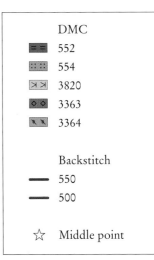

DMC	
☷ ☷	552
⠿⠿	554
⟩ ⟩	3820
◇ ◇	3363
⤬ ⤬	3364

Backstitch
—— 550
—— 500

☆ Middle point

1

Beginning in the centre of the canvas, work the cross stitch design using two strands of cotton, and the backstitch using a single strand.

2

To make up, cut 2 tag shapes out of the handmade paper, and with the craft knife, cut an opening in one. Stick the embroidered panel in the window and trim the edges of the fabric. Glue the back of the label in place.

3

Once the glue has dried, punch a hole at the end of the tag and stick the reinforcing rings on either side. Plait a length of dark green, gold and purple threads together and loop them through the hole to finish off the tag.

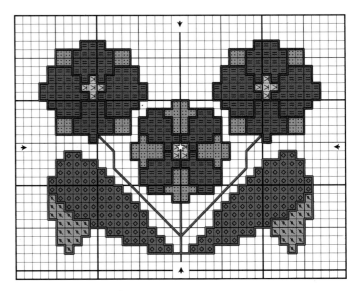

Greetings Card

1

Tack the fine calico to the back of the silk and fit into a hoop. Tack the waste canvas onto the middle of the fabric, keeping the canvas in line with the grain of the fabric. Mark the centre of the canvas. Stitch the design using 2 strands of cotton. When complete, fray and pull out the canvas threads one at a time. Press on the reverse side and trim to fit behind the opening.

2

To make up, stick tape round the inside edge of the opening and position the embroidery on top. Stick the backing card in position. Use double-sided tape to assemble because glue tends to buckle the card.

MATERIALS

20 cm / 8 in square of fine calico
20 cm / 8 in square of cream silk dupion (mid-weight silk)
tacking thread
needle
embroidery hoop
13 × 15 cm / 5 × 6 in
14-count waste canvas
stranded cotton DMC nos. 221, 223, 224, 744, 3362 and 3363
embroidery needle
scissors
craft card with an 8 × 12 cm / 3 × 4¾ in aperture
double-sided tape

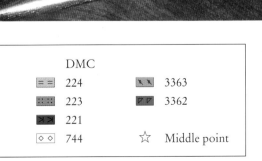

DMC		DMC	
═ ═	224	⊼ ⊼	3363
⁚⁚ ⁚⁚	223	◢ ◢	3362
◄ ◄	221		
◇ ◇	744	☆	Middle point

Handkerchief Case

*No more scrabbling in the drawer – this pretty and practical pouch with its
dainty trellis pattern will keep all your hankies tidy.*

MATERIALS

*two 53 × 20 cm / 21 × 8 in
pieces of white 36-count
evenweave linen
tacking thread
needle
embroidery hoop
stranded cotton DMC nos.
221, 223, 224, 225, 501,
502, 503, 832, 834, 839,
3032 and 3782
tapestry needle
pins
sewing machine
sewing thread
scissors
1 m / 1 yd wine-coloured
piping*

1

Tack a guideline crossways 10 cm / 4 in from one
end of the linen. Mark the centre of this line and
begin the cross stitch. The bottom of the design
is the side nearest the raw edge.

2

Work the design using a single strand of cotton
over 2 threads of linen. When the embroidery
is complete, press on the reverse side.
A magnifying glass might help.

DMC		DMC	
– –	501	5 5	225
III	502	7 7	839
1 1	503	9 9	832
2 2	221	II II	834
3 3	223	◇ ◇	3032
4 4	224	✕ ✕	3782

☆ Middle point

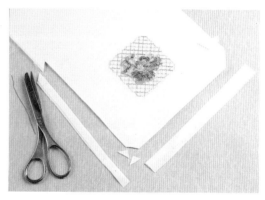

3

To make up, pin the 2 linen panels together with
the embroidery to the inside. With a 2 cm / ¾ in
seam allowance, sew all round, leaving a gap on
one side for turning. Trim the seams and across
the corners, then turn through.

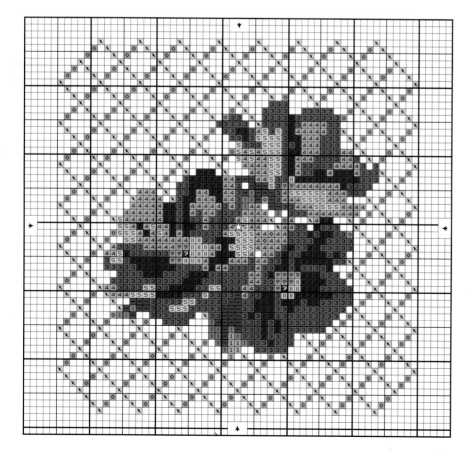

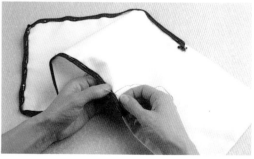

4

Fold the panel in 3 and tack along the fold
lines. Pin the piping to the inside of the front
flap and down both sides as far as the second
fold line. Turn under the ends and slip stitch
the piping in place. Slip stitch the side seams
to complete the case.

Birth Keepsake

This gift has a practical use as a pincushion but could be filled with lavender instead.

MATERIALS

15 cm / 6 in square of white
25-count Lugana, Zweigart
E3835
tacking thread
needle
embroidery hoop
stranded cotton DMC nos.
350, 47 and 3326
tapestry needle
118 small pink beads
scissors
15 cm / 6 in square of white
backing fabric
sewing machine
sewing thread
2 14 cm / 5 ½ in squares of
wadding (batting)
pins
75 cm / 30 in white
crocheted lace edging
(dipped in weak tea to
colour slightly)

1

Tack guidelines in both directions across the centre of the linen. Work the cross stitch using 3 strands of cotton over 2 threads. Once complete, sew a bead over the top of each stitch in the pink hearts. Use a double length of thread and begin with a secure knot.

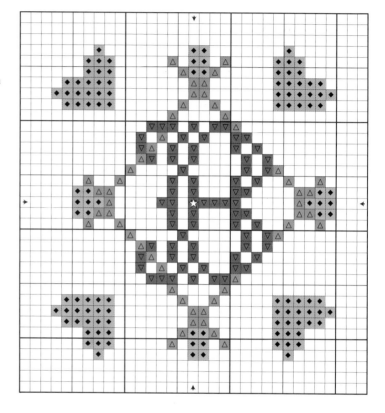

DMC		
▽▽	350	☆ Middle
△△	472	point
◆◆	3326	

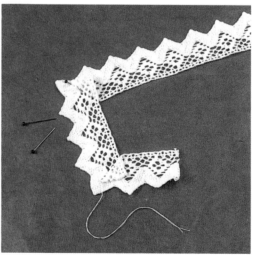

2

To make up, block the design if necessary and trim away the excess fabric leaving 4 cm / 1½ in round the cross stitch. Cut the backing fabric to match and stitch the embroidery and backing fabric together, with right sides facing, leaving a gap along one side. Trim the seams and across the corners to reduce bulk.

3

Tuck the wadding (batting) into the cushion and slip stitch to close. Mitre the corners of the lace one at a time by folding and stitching diagonally on the wrong side. Each side should be about 13 cm / 5 in long. Join the lace ends and pin round the cushion 1 cm / ½ in in from the edge. Stitch neatly in place.

Baby Birth Gift

Celebrate a baby's birth by giving the parents this very pretty arrangement in an unusual but practical container. The display incorporates double tulips, ranunculus, phlox and spray roses, with small leaves of pittosporum.

The choice of soft, subtle colours means that the arrangement is suitable for either a boy or a girl. There is also the added bonus of the beautiful scents of the phlox and dried lavender. Since the arrangement has its own container, it is particularly convenient for a recipient in hospital, avoiding, as it does, the need to find a vase. Finally, the container can be kept and used again after the life of the display.

MATERIALS

block plastic foam
scissors
small galvanized metal bucket
bunch pittosporum
15 stems pale pink 'Angelique' tulips
5 stems white spray roses
10 stems white ranunculus
10 stems white phlox
bunch dried lavender
ribbon, purple and white check

1

Soak the plastic foam in water, cut it to fit the small metal bucket and wedge it firmly in place. Cut the pittosporum to a length of 12 cm/4¾ in and clean the leaves from the lower part of the stems. Push the stems into the plastic foam to create an overall domed foliage outline within which the flowers can be arranged.

2

Cut the 'Angelique' tulips to a stem length of 10 cm/4 in and distribute them evenly throughout the foliage. Cut individual off-shoots from the main stems of the spray roses to a length of 10 cm/4 in, and arrange throughout the display, with full blooms at the centre and buds around the outside.

3

Cut the ranunculus and phlox to a stem length of 10 cm/ 4 in and distribute both throughout the display. Cut the lavender to a stem length of 12 cm/4¾ in and arrange in groups of 3 stems evenly throughout the flowers and foliage. Tie the ribbon around the bucket and finish in a generous bow.

Planted Basket for Baby

This display of pot plants in a basket makes a lovely gift to celebrate the birth of a baby. It is easy to make and is a long-lasting alternative to a cut-flower arrangement.

The combination of two simple and delicate white plants, baby cyclamen and lily-of-the-valley, gives the design charm and purity, indeed everything about it says 'baby'.

MATERIALS

*wire basket
2 handfuls Spanish moss
cellophane
scissors
3 pots miniature white
cyclamen
3 pots lily-of-the-valley
paper ribbon*

1

Line the wire basket with generous handfuls of Spanish moss, then carefully line the moss with cellophane. Trim the cellophane so that it fits neatly around the rim of the basket.

2

Remove the plants from their pots carefully. Loosen the soil and the roots a little before planting them in the basket, alternating the cyclamen with the lily-of-the-valley and adding more moss if necessary.

3

Make sure that the plants are firmly bedded in the basket. Make two small bows from the paper ribbon, smoothing open the ends, and attach one to each side of the basket at the base of the handle.

Herb Bath-bag

Enjoy a traditional herbal bath by filling a fine muslin bag with relaxing herbs, tying it to the taps and letting the hot water run through. This draw-string design means it can be re-used time after time, if you keep refilling it with new herbs. Chamomile and hops are relaxing; basil and sage are invigorating.

MATERIALS

*silky muslin, about 30 × 40 cm /
12 × 16 in
pins, needle and thread*

*scissors
fabric scraps, for casing
1 m / 39 in narrow ribbon*

*safety pin
herb bath-mix or any combination
of dried herbs*

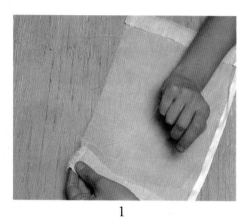

1

With right sides facing, fold over about 5 cm / 2 in of the silky muslin at both short ends, pin and stitch each side. Trim the seams. Turn right-side out.

2

Turn in and hem the raw edges of the folded-over ends.

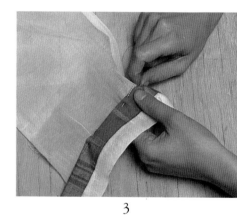

3

Cut two strips of cotton fabric about 2.5 cm / 1 in wide and as long as the width of the muslin, with about 5 mm / ¼ in extra for turnings all round. Iron a hem along both long edges. Turn in and hem the ends, then pin one casing on the right side of the muslin so the bottom edge of the casing lines up with the hem line. Neatly stitch the casing in place along both long seams. Repeat with the other casing.

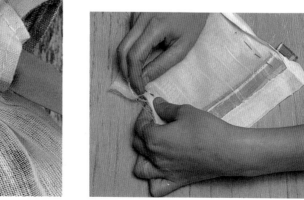

4

With right sides together, fold the muslin in half so the casings line up. Stitch the side seams from the bottom edge of the casing to the bottom edge of the bag. Trim the seams.

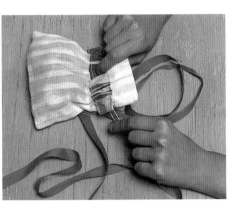

5

Cut the ribbon in half, attach a safety pin to one end and use this to thread the ribbon through the casing so both ends finish up at the same side. Remove the safety pin.

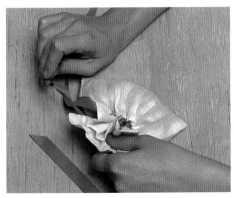

6

Attach the safety pin to one end of the other piece of ribbon and thread it through the casing in the other direction so the ends finish up at the other side. Fill with herbs ready for use.

Shell Pot

Decorate a flowerpot with shells and some old netting, and then use it to hold plants, pencils, paintbrushes, strings, ribbon, or any paraphernalia that needs to be kept in check. It's a pretty and inexpensive way to make a very special container.

MATERIALS

small net bag
flowerpot, 18 cm / 7 in tall
scissors
hot glue gun and glue sticks
thick string
small cowrie shells
cockle shells
starfish or similar central motif

1

Slip the net bag over the flowerpot and trim the top edge. Secure it by gluing on a length of string.

2

Using a glue gun, position a row of cowrie shells along the top edge.

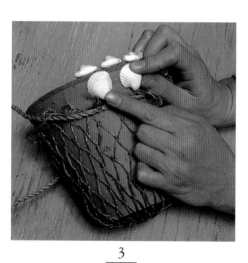

3

Glue cockle shells around the rim; position the starfish and four cockle shells at the front.

Shell Box

A simple brown-paper box takes on a South-Seas feel when decorated with half-cowries. Available from craft shops, their flattened bottoms make them easy to stick to surfaces. Here, some have also been strung together to make a toggle for fastening.

MATERIALS

hot glue gun and glue sticks
raffia
small buff box
half-cowrie shells
upholstery needle

1

Glue a loop of raffia from the bottom of the box, up the back and along the top.

2

Tie half-cowries into a bunch on a length of raffia, tying each one in separately. Leave a short length of raffia free. Pierce the front of the box with an upholstery needle and thread the raffia through. Knot it on the inside.

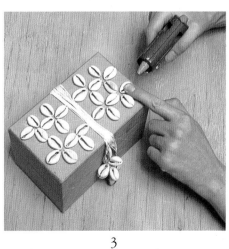

3

Glue on a pattern of half-cowries to decorate the outside of the box.

Shell Candle Centrepiece

An old flowerpot, scallop shells gleaned from the fishmonger or kitchen and smaller shells picked up from the beach make up a fabulous, Venus-inspired table-centrepiece. Either put a candle in the centre, as here, or fill it with dried fruits or flowers.

MATERIALS

hot glue gun and glue sticks
8 curved scallop shells
flowerpot, 18 cm / 7 in tall
bag of cockle shells
4 flat scallop shells
newspaper, florist's foam or
other packing material
saucer
candle
raffia

1

Generously apply hot glue to the inside lower edge of a large curved scallop shell. Hold it in place on the rim of the pot for a few seconds until it is firmly stuck. Continue sticking shells to the top of the pot, arranging them so they overlap slightly, until the whole of the rim has been covered.

2

In the same way, glue a cockle shell where two scallops join. Continue all around the pot.

3

Place another row of cockles at the joins of the first row. Glue flat scallop shells face upwards to the bottom of the pot, first at the front, then at the back, and then the two sides, to ensure the pot stands straight.

4

Fill the pot with packing material and place a saucer on top of this. Stand a candle on the saucer.

5

Tie raffia around the pot where it joins the stand.

6

Decorate the stand with a few more cockles, if you like. Stand a few more curved scallop shells inside the original row to create a fuller, more petalled shape.

Shell Mirror

The subtle rose-pinks of ordinary scallop shells, picked up from the fishmonger, make for an easy, eye-catching mirror surround that's also environmentally friendly. Here, four large ones have been used at the corners with smaller ones filling in the sides.

MATERIALS

*sandpaper
mirror in wooden frame
paint
paintbrush
4 large flat scallop shells
hot glue gun and glue sticks
10 small flat scallop shells
seagrass string
2 metal eyelets*

1

Sand down and paint the mirror frame with the colour of your choice.

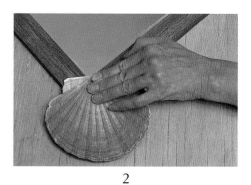

2

Position the large scallop shells at the corners of the mirror, using the hot glue.

3

In the same way, glue three of the smaller scallop shells to each side of the mirror.

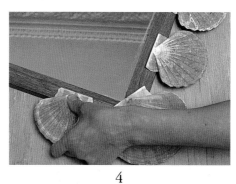

4

Attach two of the smaller scallop shells to the top of the mirror and two to the bottom.

5

Plait three lengths of seagrass string to make a hanger.

6

Screw metal eyelets into each side of the frame at the back, and tie the hanger on to these.

Filigree Leaf Wrap

Even the most basic brown parcel-paper can take on a very special look. Use a gilded skeletonized leaf and gold twine in combination with brown paper; chunky coir string would give a more robust look.

MATERIALS

picture framer's wax gilt
large skeletonized leaf
brown paper
sticky tape
gold twine
hot glue gun and glue sticks,
if necessary

1

Rub wax gilt into the skeletonized leaf.

2

Wrap the parcel in the brown paper and rub gilt wax on to the corners. Tie the parcel with gold twine, bringing the two ends together and tying a knot. Fray the ends to create a tassle effect. Slip the leaf under the twine, securing it with glue at each end if necessary.

Fruit and Foliage Gift-wraps

Here, gilded brown parcel-paper provides a fitting background for a decoration of leaves and dried fruit slices.

MATERIALS

brown paper
sticky tape
picture framer's wax gilt
seagrass string
hot glue gun and glue sticks
dried fruit slices
preserved leaves

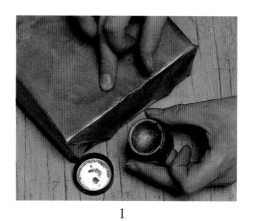

1

Wrap the parcel with brown paper and rub in gilt wax, paying special attention to the corners.

2

Tie the parcel with seagrass string, and then glue a different dried fruit or leaf to each quarter.

Tissue Rosette Gift-wrap

*Tissue papers make a fabulous foundation for any gift-wrapping; they come in
a glorious array of colours, and they softly take to any shape.*

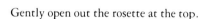

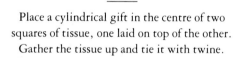

1

Place a cylindrical gift in the centre of two
squares of tissue, one laid on top of the other.
Gather the tissue up and tie it with twine.

2

Gently open out the rosette at the top.

Lavender Tissue Gift-wrap

*Bunches of lavender add a real country touch to tissue gift-wrap,
and become part of the gift.*

1

Make two bunches of lavender and tie them
with twine to form a cross.

2

Wrap the parcel in the darker toned tissue
paper, and then wrap it with the paler tissue,
cut to form an envelope. Glue the lavender
to the front of the parcel.

Dried Flower Gift Wrap

To make a present extra special why not make the wrapping part of the gift? The display is effectively a dried flower corsage but used to embellish gift wrapping.

It takes a little time to produce but its natural, warm, earthy colours make this a delightful enhancement well worth the effort, and something to keep.

MATERIALS

dried sunflower head
scissors
stub wires
small dried pomegranate
3 small pieces dried fungi
(graded in size)
3 slices dried orange
(graded in size)
silver stub wires
florist's tape
gift-wrapped present
raffia

__1__

Cut the sunflower to a stem length of 2.5 cm/1 in and double leg mount on a stub wire. Single leg mount the pomegranates on stub wire. Double leg mount the small pieces of fungi on stub wires and mount the orange slices on silver stub wires.

__2__

Wrap all the wired materials with tape, then attach the 3 orange slices to one side of the sunflower and pomegranate, then attach the 3 layers of fungi on the other side. Bind all these in place using the silver wire or reel wire if you prefer.

__3__

Trim the wire stems to a length of 5 cm/2 in and tape together with florist's tape. Tie the raffia around the present and push the wired stem of the decoration under the raffia knot. Secure in place with another stub wire or pieces of double-sided tape.

Dried Flowers as a Gift

This is a great way to present dried flowers as a gift. Treat them as you would a tied bouquet of cut fresh flowers, prettily wrapped in tissue paper and tied with a large bow.

The deep pink mixture of exotic and garden flowers – protea and amaranthus with peonies and larkspur – makes this a floral gift anyone would be thrilled to receive.

MATERIALS

10 small dried pink
Protea compacta *buds*
*10 stems dried pink
larkspur
10 stems dried pink
peonies
10 stems dried green
amaranthus
raffia
scissors
2 sheets blue tissue paper
pink ribbon*

1

Lay out the dried materials so that they are all easily accessible. Start the bouquet with a dried protea held in your hand, add a stem of larkspur, a stem of peony and a stem of amaranthus, all the while turning the bunch with every addition.

2

Continue until all the dried materials have been used. Tie with raffia at the binding point – where the stems cross each other. Trim the stem ends so that their length is approximately one-third of the overall height of the finished bouquet.

3

Lay the sheets of tissue paper on a flat surface and place the bouquet diagonally across the tissue. Wrap the tissue paper around the flowers, overlapping it at the front. Tie securely at the binding point with a ribbon and form a large, floppy bow.

Leafy Pictures

Delicate skeletonized leaves come in such breathtakingly exquisite forms that they deserve to be shown off. Mount them on hand-made papers and frame them to make simple yet stunning natural collages.

MATERIALS

wooden picture frame
sandpaper
paint
paintbrush
backing paper
pencil
scissors
skeletonized leaf
picture framer's wax gilt
hot glue gun and glue sticks
mounting paper

1

Take the frame apart and sand it down to provide a key before painting. A translucent colourwash has been used for painting here, but any paint will do.

2

Allow the paint to dry, then sand the paint back so you're left with a wooden frame with shading in the mouldings, plus a veil of colour on the surface.

3

Use the hardboard back of the frame as a template for the backing paper. Draw around it with a pencil to form a cutting line.

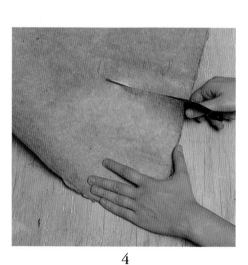

4

Cut the backing paper out.

5

Prepare the leaf by rubbing with picture framer's wax gilt. This does take a little time as the gilt has to be well worked in.

6

Stick the backing paper on the frame back, glue the mounting paper in the centre and attach the leaf on to that. Here, the leaf is centred with the stalk breaking the edge of the mounting paper. Finally, put the frame back together.

Spicy Pomander

*Pomanders were originally nature's own air fresheners. The traditional
orange pomanders are fairly tricky to do, because the critical drying process can
so easily go wrong, leading to mouldy oranges. This one, made of cloves and
cardamom pods offers none of those problems, and makes a refreshing change
in soft muted colours.*

MATERIALS

*cloves
florist's dry foam ball,
about 7.5 cm / 3 in diameter
hot glue gun and glue sticks
green cardamom pods
raffia
florist's stub wire*

1

Start by making a single line of cloves all
around the circumference of the ball.
Make another one in the other direction,
so you have divided the ball into quarters.

2

Make a line of cloves on both sides of the
original lines to make broad bands of cloves
quartering the ball.

3

Starting at the top of the first quarter,
glue cardamom pods over the foam,
methodically working in rows to create a neat
effect. Repeat on the other three quarters.

4

Tie a bow in the centre of a length of raffia.
Pass a stub wire through the knot and
twist the ends together.

5

Fix the bow to the top of the ball
using the stub wire.

6

Join the two loose ends in a knot
for hanging the pomander.

Tulip Pomander

In Elizabethan times pomanders were filled with herbs or scented flowers and carried to perfume the air. Today the pomander is more likely to be a bridesmaid's accessory.

The pomander illustrated does not boast exotic aromas but it does have a pleasing variety of surface textures, ranging from the spiky inner petals of double tulips through the beady black berries of myrtle to the softness of grey moss, all set against bands of smooth satin ribbon. It would be a charming alternative to the bridesmaid's traditional posy.

MATERIALS

plastic foam ball
ribbon
scissors
20 heads 'Appleblossom'
double tulips
bunch myrtle
stub wires
good handful
reindeer moss

1

Soak the foam ball in water. Tie the ribbon around the ball, starting at the top and crossing at the bottom, and then tying at the top to divide the ball into four equal segments. Make sure there is enough ribbon to tie into a bow.

2

Cut the tulips to a stem length of about 2.5 cm/1 in and push into the foam in vertical lines at the centre of each segment. Hold the tulip heads gently while positioning them on the foam ball to avoid the heads breaking off.

3

Push sprigs of myrtle into the foam to form lines on either side of each line of tulips.

4

Use bent stub wires to cover all remaining exposed areas of the foam ball with moss.

Cinnamon and Orange Ring

The warm colours, spicy smell and culinary content of this small decorated ring make it perfect for the wall of a kitchen. The display is not complicated to make but requires nimble fingers to handle the very small pieces of cinnamon used. These pieces have to be tightly packed together to achieve the right effect and attaching so much cinnamon to the plastic foam may cause it to collapse. To prevent this happening, you can glue the foam ring to a piece of card cut to the same outline before you begin.

MATERIALS

glue gun and glue sticks
5 dried oranges
plastic foam ring for
dried flowers, 13 cm /
5¾ in diameter
20 cinnamon sticks

1

Apply glue to the bases of the dried oranges and space them evenly around the foam ring. Break the cinnamon sticks into 2–4 cm /¾-1½ in pieces.

2

Apply glue to the bottom of the pieces of cinnamon and push them into the foam between the dried oranges, keeping them close together.

3

Glue a line of the cinnamon pieces around both the inside and outside edges of the ring to cover the plastic foam completely.

Classic Orange and Clove Pomander

This classic pomander starts as fresh material that, as you use it, dries into a beautiful old-fashioned decoration with a warm, spicy smell evocative of mulled wine and the festive season. Make several pomanders using different ribbons and display them in a bowl, hang them around the house, use them as Christmas decorations or even hang them in the airing-cupboard to perfume your sheets and towels.

MATERIALS

3 small firm oranges
3 types of ribbon
scissors
cloves

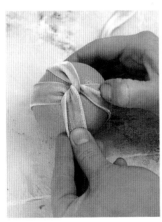

1	2	3
Tie a ribbon around an orange, crossing it over at the base so that it neatly quarters the orange.	Finish off at the top of the orange by tying the ribbon into a bow. Clip the ends of the ribbon to prevent it from fraying.	Starting at the edges of the areas, push the sharp ends of the exposed cloves into the orange and continue until it is completely covered.

Red Tied Sheaf

A tied sheaf of flowers arranged in the hand makes an attractive and informal wall decoration. To make a successful wall hanging, the sheaf must be made with a flat back, while at the same time it should have a profiled front to add visual interest. This richly coloured display would make a wonderful house-warming gift.

The demanding aspect of the construction of the sheaf is the technique of spiralling the materials in your hand. But this display is relatively small, which simplifies the task.

MATERIALS

50 stems dried lavender
10 stems Protea compacta *buds*
10 stems natural ti tree
15 stems dried red roses
twine
scissors
satin ribbon, 5 cm / 2 in

1

Lay out the materials so that they are easily accessible and separate the lavender into 10 smaller groups. Hold the longest protea in your hand, and behind it add a slightly longer stem of ti tree, then hold rose stems to either side of the protea, both slightly shorter than the first. Continue adding materials in a regular repeating sequence to the growing bunch in your hand, spiralling the stems as you do so.

2

When all the materials have been used, tie the sheath with twine at the binding point. Trim the stems so that they make up about one-third of the overall length of the sheaf.

3

To finish the display make a separate ribbon bow and attach it to the sheaf at the binding point.

Rose and Clove Pomander

This pomander is a decadent display of rose heads massed in a ball. But it has a secret: cloves hidden between the rose heads, giving the pomander its lasting spicy perfume. It relies for its impact on the use of large quantities of tightly packed flowers, all of the same type and colour.

1

Fold the ribbon in half and double leg mount its cut ends together with a stub wire. To form a ribbon handle, push the wires right through the plastic foam ball so that they come out the other end, and pull the projecting wires so that the double leg mounted part of the ribbon becomes firmly embedded in the plastic foam. Turn the excess wire back into the foam.

Almost profligate in its use of materials, this pomander is quick to make and would be a wonderful and very special gift.

MATERIALS

*ribbon 40 × 2.5 cm /
16 × 1 in stub wire
plastic foam ball for dried
flowers, approximately
10 cm / 4 in diameter
scissors
100 stems dried roses
200 cloves*

2

Cut the stems of the dried rose heads to a length of approximately 2.5 cm / 1 in. Starting at the top of the plastic foam ball, push the stems of the dried rose heads into the foam to form a tightly packed circle around the base of the ribbon handle. As you work, push a clove into the plastic foam between each rose head. Continue forming concentric circles of rose heads and cloves around the plastic foam ball until it is completely covered.

Herbal Tablepiece

Extremely strong-smelling herbs should be avoided for table centres because their fragrance may overpower the flavour of the meal. However, gently scented herbs make a delightful table decoration.

*shallow basket without handle
2 blocks florist's foam for dried
flowers
florist's wire
florist's tape
scissors
2 bunches cardoon thistles
3 large ivory candles
bunches of dried herbs, where
possible in flower, including oregano,
lavender, marjoram and fennel*

Caution: make sure that this arrangement is never left unattended while the candles are alight.

1

Fill the basket with foam, wedging it into position. Group the cardoon heads into 3 positions in the foam. Make hairpins from lengths of wire, and tape 3 hairpins around the base of each candle. Place the candles into the foam.

2

Wire small bunches of lavender and marjoram, and spread evenly around the arrangement. Place the fennel flower heads in the arrangement singly or wired together in groups, depending upon the space you wish to fill.

Dried Herbal Topiary Tree

Topiary trees are an attractive way of displaying flowers and natural objects. This design includes small terracotta pots, which add to the textural interest in the top of the tree.

MATERIALS

*large terracotta pot for the base
cement or plaster of Paris
piece of tree branch for the trunk
13 cm / 5 in ball of florist's foam for
dried flowers
small pieces of similar foam
2 large bunches of glycerined copper
beech foliage or other preserved
foliage
scissors
heavy-gauge florist's wire
wire cutters
12 miniature terracotta pots
2 bunches golden rod
light florist's wire
hot glue gun (optional)
2 bunches poppy heads*

1

Cover the hole in the large terracotta pot and half fill with wet cement or plaster of Paris. As the cement begins to harden, stand the branch in the pot to form the trunk. Leave to dry for at least 48 hours before proceeding to the next step.

2

Press the foam ball on to the trunk, making sure it is firmly in place, but not so far down that the trunk comes out the other side of the ball. Cover the cement in the base with pieces of foam.

3

Cover the ball and base with pieces of copper beech or other preserved foliage. Thread heavy-gauge wire through the holes in the small pots and make a stem so they can be attached to the tree and pressed into the foam.

4

Arrange the pots through the tree and base, and fill with small wired bunches of golden rod, trimming with scissors where needed. These can be glued into position if necessary. Finally, add the poppy heads.

Herbal Christmas Wreath

Orange slices can be dried on a wire rack in an oven at the lowest possible setting for several hours until they are crisp. They should then be carefully varnished with a clear, matt varnish so that they cannot reabsorb moisture from the atmosphere.

MATERIALS

*few stems fresh holly
2 sprays fresh conifer
scissors
hot glue gun
wreath ring, approximately 23 cm /
9 in in diameter
gold spray paint
5 cm / 2 in terracotta pot
broken pieces of terracotta pot
7 ears of wheat, sprayed gold
small bunch dried sage
small bunch oregano
florist's wire
3 dried orange slices*

1

Attach the holly and conifer to the ring using the hot glue gun. Cover approximately half the ring.

2

In a well-ventilated area, spray a little gold paint on to the pot and pieces of pot and glue them to the design. Add the ears of wheat. Make small bunches of sage and tuck those among the pieces of broken pot.

3

Make a chunky bunch of the dried oregano, wiring it together. Glue into the main pot in the centre of the design. Cut the orange slices into quarters and glue those into the arrangement. The fresh ingredients will dry on the wreath and look most attractive.

Dried Herbal Posy

This posy could be given as a present or to say 'thank you'. It would also make a very pretty dressing table decoration. The ingredients are dried, so it can be made well in advance or you could make a few to have ready to give to guests.

MATERIALS

small bunch dried red roses
florist's wire
small bunch alchemilla
small bunch marjoram
cotton posy frill, deep pink
3 sprays dried bay
hot glue gun
florist's tape
scissors
ribbon, as preferred

1

Start with a small cluster of red roses, binding them with wire to form a centre. Add some alchemilla, binding gently but firmly in the same spot.

2

Bind in some marjoram and then more red roses and alchemilla, until you are happy with the size of the posy. Carefully push the stems of the paper posy through the centre of the posy frill.

3

Separate the bay leaves from the stems and glue them in, one at a time, through the arrangement and around the edge as a border.

4

Push the posy frill up towards the flowers and fasten with tape. Tie ribbon around the stem of the posy and make a bow.

Bath Bags

These are much more fun than putting commercial bubble bath into the water. Tie them over the taps and make sure the hot running water is going through them – this will release lovely herbal scents that relax and comfort you.

INGREDIENTS

3 × 23 cm / 9 in diameter circles of
muslin
6 tbsp bran
1 tbsp lavender flowers
1 tbsp chamomile flowers
1 tbsp rosemary tips
3 small rubber bands
3 m / 3 yd narrow ribbon or twine

1

Place 2 tbsp bran in the centre of each circle of muslin. Add the lavender to one bag, the chamomile to a second and the rosemary to the third, mixing the herbs through the bran.

2

Gather each circle of material up and close with a rubber band. Then tie a reasonable length of ribbon or twine around each bag to make a loop so that the bag can be hung from the hot tap in the stream of water.

Herb Corsages

Making your own buttonhole or corsage is easy. Tiny posy frills are obtainable from specialist floral suppliers or you could use the centre of a small paper doily.

MATERIALS

medium-sized flower
sprig of any herb with attractive leaves
thin florist's wire
miniature posy frill or cut-down doily
florist's tape

1

For a centrepiece, you could use a rose or small spray carnation. wrap some herb foliage around it – fresh green parsley would look good – and then bind it tightly with thin wire.

2

Push the stems through the centre of the frill and tape them together, covering the stems all the way down. Other combinations could include rosemary, sage, lavender or box.

Scented Valentine Heart

Valentine gifts in the shape of a heart are always popular. This heart-shaped gift box with dried flower and herb decoration on the lid is accompanied by a matching wreath made with fresh leaves and flowers that remain attractive when they dry.

MATERIALS

heart-shaped box
broad and narrow ribbon
hot glue gun
5 dried roses
dried bay leaves
bunch dried golden rod
heart-shaped wreath form
houttuynia leaves
'Minuet' roses
sprig fresh lavender

1

Start decorating the gift box by making a large bow with broad ribbon. Then stick the dried ingredients on to the box to resemble a bunch of flowers. Stick the bow on top.

2

Wrap some narrow ribbon around the wreath form and secure with glue. Add a few houttyuynia leaves (this variety is *H. cordata*), some 'Minuet' roses and fresh lavender. These could be attached with wire instead of glue if you prefer.

Herb-decorated Crackers

Home-made touches are important at Christmas, as they add the final touch to a family celebration. These crackers are easy to decorate and could be made by adults and children together. Buy ready-decorated crackers and remove the commercial trimming.

MATERIALS

crackers
narrow ribbon, as preferred
scissors
small sprigs of various herbs,
pretzels, gilded rosehips
hot glue gun or general-purpose
adhesive

1

Tie the ends of the crackers with ribbon, making attractive bows.

2

Make small posies of herbs and glue them to the central part of the crackers. Add pretzels and gilded rosehips.

Scented Pressed Herb Diary

A notebook or diary can be scented by placing it in a box with a strong lavender sachet, or a cotton-wool ball sprinkled with a few drops of essential oil. Leave it in the sealed box for a month or so to impart a sweet, lingering fragrance. Try to find a very plain diary or notebook which does not have lettering or decoration on the cover, as these would spoil the design. Use a plastic film made for covering books.

MATERIALS

pressed leaves and flowers, such as borage flowers, alchemilla flowers and small leaves, daisies, single roses and forget-me-nots
plain diary or notebook
tweezers
large tapestry needle
white latex adhesive
clear plastic film
iron and cloth pad (optional)

1

Start by arranging a selection of pressed leaves on the front of the diary or notebook, using the tweezers for positioning.

2

Continue to build up your design by adding the pressed flower heads.

3

Once you are happy with the design stick it down, using a large tapestry needle and latex adhesive. Slide the needle into the glue and then, without moving the design, place a small amount of glue under each leaf and petal so that they are secure. Cover with clear film. Some kinds of film needs heating, and you should iron gently with a cloth pad between the film and the iron.

Pressed Herb Cards

A home-made card is always one that will be treasured long after the occasion has passed. Although it takes time and trouble to make your own cards, it is always worth the effort to give someone something with your personal touch.

MATERIALS

pressed herbs and flowers, such as blue cornflower, ivy, rosemary and borage
blank greetings card
large tapestry needle
white latex adhesive
clear plastic film
iron and cloth pad (optional)

1

Arrange a selection of pressed herbs and flowers on the front of the card, using tweezers to position them.

2

When the design is complete, stick it down. Using a large tapestry needle, slide small dabs of adhesive beneath the herbs and flowers without altering their position. Cover with a clear film. If the film needs heating, iron gently with a cloth pad between the film and the iron.

Bath-time Bottle

*Recycle a glass bottle containing home-made lotion and decorate it with
corrugated card in gem-like colours for a real impact.*

MATERIALS

*scissors
coloured corrugated card
flower-water bottle
hot glue gun and glue sticks
coloured raffia*

1	2
Cut the corrugated card to size, and then glue in position around the bottle. Tie with raffia.	Make a matching label from corrugated card, and tie it on using raffia.

Bath-time Treat Jar

*Decorate a jar of lotion to complement the bottle, using brilliantly
coloured fine corrugated card. Royal blue and emerald green make a rich
combination that could be used for both men and women.*

MATERIALS

*scissors
coloured corrugated card
baby-food jar
hot glue gun and glue sticks
twine*

1	2
Cut the corrugated card to size, and then glue in place around the jar. Tie the twine around the jar.	Cut a piece of corrugated card to fit the top of the lid and glue it in place. Glue twine to cover the side of the lid.

Chamomile and Honey Mask

Although this mask makes you look a little strange while it is on your face, it smooths and softens skin beautifully. Chamomile flowers are usually easy to obtain from a health food shop as they are often used for making chamomile tea.

INGREDIENTS

*1 tbsp dried chamomile flowers
175 ml / 6 fl oz boiling water
2 tbsp bran
1 tsp clear honey, warmed*

1

Pour the boiling water over the chamomile flowers and allow them to stand for 30 minutes. Then strain the infusion and discard the chamomile flowers.

2

Mix 3 tbsp of the liquid with the bran and honey and rub this mixture over your face. Leave for at least 10 minutes, then rinse off with warm water.

Tansy Skin Tonic

Tansy leaves smell fairly strong, but this tonic will invigorate your skin, especially if you keep the bottle in the refrigerator. Splash on this cool herbal liquid to start the day.

INGREDIENTS

large handful tansy leaves
150 ml / ¼ pint water
150 ml / ¼ pint milk

1

Put the leaves, water and milk in a small pan and bring to the boil. Simmer for 15 minutes, then allow to cool in the pan.

2

Strain the tonic into a bottle. Keep the mixture in the refrigerator, and apply cold to the skin as a soothing toner or tonic.

Feverfew Complexion Milk

Feverfew grows prolifically in the garden, self-seeding all over the herb beds, and this is a welcome use for some of this over-enthusiastic plant. The milk will moisturize dry skin, help to fade blemishes and discourage blackheads.

Feverfew can be cultivated easily; it is especially pretty grown in tubs and pots in the greenhouse or conservatory.

Hang bunches of flowers upside down and leave to air dry; use as a decorative addition to dried flower arrangements.

INGREDIENTS

large handful feverfew leaves
300 ml / ½ pint milk

1

Put the leaves and milk in a small saucepan and simmer for 20 minutes.

2

Allow the mixture to cool in the pan then strain into a bottle. Keep it in the refrigerator.

Fennel Cleanser

Fennel is another herb that self-seeds all over the garden, so once you have planted it supplies will be no problem. The leaves have an aniseed aroma. This mixture gently but thoroughly cleanses the day's grime away.

The tall, graceful heads of fennel seeds add height to a cottage herb garden. The seeds are valued for their distinctive aroma. In Victorian times the seeds came to symbolize the virtue of strength.

At one time, fennel seeds were combined with those of dill and caraway in little sacks or purses, to be chewed at prayer meetings to quell hunger pangs: they were known as 'meeting seeds'.

INGREDIENTS

1 tbsp fennel seed
250 ml / 8 fl oz boiling water
1 tsp honey
2 tbsp buttermilk

1

Lightly crush the fennel seeds, pour on the boiling water and allow to infuse for about 30 minutes.

2

Strain the cooled liquid into a small bowl and add the honey and buttermilk. Transfer to a clean bottle and keep the mixture refrigerated.

Parsley Hair Tonic

Parsley stimulates the scalp and gets the circulation going, which aids hair growth and adds shine. Parsley is cultivated in the garden in numerous forms, including curly, plain and turnip-rooted. It is one of the most versatile herbs, and no herb garden should be without at least one plant.

INGREDIENTS

*large handful parsley sprigs
2 tbsp water*

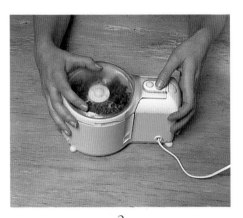

1

Place the parsley sprigs and water in a food processor.

2

Process until ground to a smooth purée. Apply the green lotion to the scalp, then wrap your head in a warm towel and leave for about 1 hour before shampooing as normal.

Lemon Verbena Hair Rinse

Add a delicious fragrance to your hair with this rinse. It will also stimulate the pores and circulation. Lemon verbena is worth growing in the garden, if only so that you can walk past and pick a wonderfully scented leaf.

INGREDIENTS

*handful lemon verbena leaves
250 ml / 8 fl oz boiling water*

1

Pour the boiling water over the lemon verbena leaves and leave to soak for 1 hour.

2

Strain the mixture and discard the leaves. Pour this rinse over your hair after conditioning.

Chamomile Conditioning Rinse

Chamomile flowers help to keep blonde hair a bright, clear colour. They will not lift the colour in hair that is medium to dark, but will help to brighten naturally fair hair, as well as leaving a pleasant fragrance.

INGREDIENTS

125 ml / 4 fl oz chamomile flowers
600 ml / 1 pint water
handful scented geranium leaves

1

Place the flowers and water in a saucepan and bring to the boil. Simmer for approximately 15 minutes.

2

While the liquid is still hot, strain on to the scented geranium leaves. Leave to soak for 30–40 minutes. Strain again, this time into a bottle. Use the mixture after shampooing.

Rosemary Hair Tonic

Rosemary is an excellent substitute for mildly medicated shampoos, and this tonic also helps to control greasy hair and enhances the shine and natural colour.

INGREDIENTS

250 ml / 8 fl oz fresh rosemary tips
1.2 litres / 2 pints bottled water

1

Put the ingredients in a saucepan and bring to the boil. Simmer for approximately 20 minutes, then allow to cool in the pan.

2

Strain the mixture and store it in a clean bottle. Use after shampooing the hair.

Dill Aftershave

Most recipes are for fragrances for women, so here is one for men. It is best kept in the refrigerator so that the cool liquid has a bracing effect as well as smelling good.

50 g / 2 oz dill seed
1 tbsp honey
600 ml / 1 pint bottled water
1 tbsp distilled witch hazel

1

Place the dill seed, honey and water in a small saucepan and bring to the boil. Simmer for about 20 minutes.

2

Allow to cool in the pan, then add the witch hazel. Strain the cooled mixture into a bottle and refrigerate.

Lavender Bubble Bath

There is no need to buy commercially made bubble baths again. This fragrance is quite delicious and so simple to make that you can make some spares as gifts for friends and family – you will be in great demand!

bunch lavender
clean wide-necked jar, with screw top
large bottle clear organic shampoo
5 drops oil of lavender

1

Place the bunch of lavender head downwards in the jar. If the stalks are longer than the jar cut them down, as it is the flowers that do the work. Add the shampoo and the lavender oil.

2

Close the jar and place on a sunny window sill for 2–3 weeks, shaking occasionally.

3

Strain the liquid and re-bottle. Use about 1 tbsp in a bath.

Lemon Grass, Coriander and Clove Bath

If you are suffering from stiff limbs after excessive exercise, this bath will help stimulate the circulation and relieve suffering in joints and muscles.

INGREDIENTS

2 tbsp almond oil
2 drops lemon grass oil
2 drops coriander oil
2 drops clove oil

1

Carefully measure the almond oil into a small dish.

2

Slowly drop in the other essential oils. Mix all the ingredients and pour into the bath while the water is running.

Lavender and Marjoram Bath

This bath mixture has the added bonus of moisturizing the skin while it gently soothes away cares and troubles. The essential oils induce sleep. To enhance the effect, you could add a bath bag containing fresh lavender and marjoram to the water.

Lavender oil is the most useful of all the essential oils, and perhaps the safest. Allergic reaction is virtually unknown and, unlike many of the other essential oils, it is safe to apply it directly to the skin.

It can help to promote sleep – sprinkle a few drops on to the pillow, or on to a handkerchief placed on the pillow, for adults and children to enjoy untroubled rest.

It is also excellent for treating burns, stings, scalds and minor wounds. Deter flying insects by rubbing the essential oil into uncovered parts of the body, such as hands and feet, on a warm evening when sitting outside.

INGREDIENTS

2 tbsp almond oil
7 drops lavender oil
3 drops marjoram oil

2

Mix all the ingredients together and pour them into the bath while the water is running, then have a long soothing soak.

1

Measure out all the ingredients into a small dish or bowl.

COUNTRY
Cooking

LIZ TRIGG

Spring Recipes

Spring brings the first of the year's tender young vegetables, and there are plenty of tempting recipes to make the most of seasonal produce. Treat yourself to a zesty lemon cake for an Easter tea or delicious spring chicken with garlic for a spring lunch.

Warm Chicken Salad with Sesame and Coriander

INGREDIENTS

4 medium chicken breasts, boned and
skinned
225 g / 8 oz mange-tout
2 heads decorative lettuce
3 carrots, peeled and julienned
170 g / 6 oz button mushrooms, sliced
6 rashers of bacon, fried

For the dressing
115 ml / 4 fl oz lemon juice
2 tbsp wholegrain mustard
250 ml / 8 fl oz olive oil
65 ml / 2½ fl oz sesame oil
1 tsp coriander seeds, crushed
1 tbsp fresh coriander leaves
chopped, to garnish

Serves 6

1

Mix all the dressing ingredients in a bowl.
Place the chicken in a dish and pour on
half the dressing. Refrigerate overnight.

2

Cook the mange-tout for 2 minutes in
boiling water, then cool under running
cold water to stop them cooking any
further. Tear the lettuces into small pieces
and mix all the other salad ingredients and
the chopped bacon together.

3

Grill the chicken breasts until cooked
through, then slice them on the diagonal
into quite thin pieces. Divide between the
bowls of salad, and add some dressing to
each dish. Combine quickly and scatter
some fresh coriander over each bowl.

Spinach and Roquefort Pancakes

INGREDIENTS

115 g / 4 oz plain flour
2 eggs
5 tbsp sunflower oil
a little salt
250 ml / 8 fl oz milk
45 g / 1½ oz / 3 tbsp butter for frying

For the filling
1 kg / 2 lb frozen spinach, thawed
225 g / 8 oz cream cheese
225 g / 8 oz Roquefort cheese
2 tbsp chopped walnuts
2 tsp chervil

For the sauce
50 g / 2 oz / 4 tbsp butter
50 g / 2 oz flour
600 ml / 1 pint milk
1 tsp wholegrain mustard
170 g / 6 oz Roquefort cheese
1 tbsp finely chopped walnuts
1 tbsp fresh chopped chervil, to garnish

Makes 16

1

Process the flour, eggs, oil and salt, slowly
adding milk until the mixture has the
consistency of single cream. (You may not
need to add all the milk.) Let the batter
rest in the refrigerator for 1 hour. Put 1 tsp
of the butter into a frying pan, and once it
has melted swirl it around to coat the
surface of the pan.

3

Cook the spinach over a low heat for about
15 minutes. Strain off the water and let the
spinach cool. Process in a food processor
with the cream cheese and Roquefort until
smooth. Turn into a bowl and add half the
walnuts and chervil.

2

Drop a large tablespoonful of batter into
the pan and tilt to spread it around evenly.
Cook until golden brown on the bottom,
then turn and cook briefly on the other
side. Lay the pancake on a wire rack. Cook
the others in the same way.

4

Preheat the oven to 190°C/375°F/Gas
Mark 5. Fill all the pancakes and place in a
shallow ovenproof dish, rolled tightly and
in rows. Make the sauce by melting the
butter, adding the flour and cooking for a
minute or two. Add the milk and stir
constantly until the sauce comes to the
boil. Stir in all the other ingredients except
the chervil. Pour the sauce over the
pancakes and bake for 20 minutes. Serve
immediately, garnished with chervil and
the remaining walnuts.

Leek and Monkfish with Thyme Sauce

Monkfish is a well-known fish now, thanks to its excellent flavour and firm texture.

INGREDIENTS

1 kg / 2 lb monkfish, cubed
salt and pepper
75 g / 3 oz / generous ⅓ cup butter
4 leeks, sliced
1 tbsp flour
150 ml / ¼ pint / ⅔ cup fish or
vegetable stock
2 tsp finely chopped fresh thyme,
plus more to garnish
juice of 1 lemon
150 ml / ¼ pint / ⅔ cup single cream
radicchio, to garnish

Serves 4

1

Season the fish to taste. Melt about a third of the butter in a pan, and fry the fish for a short time. Put to one side.

2

Fry the leeks in the pan with another third of the butter until they have softened. Put these to one side with the fish.

3

In a saucepan, melt the rest of the butter, add the butter from the pan, stir in the flour, and add the stock. As the sauce thickens, add the thyme and lemon juice.

4

Return the leeks and monkfish to the pan and cook gently for a few minutes. Add the cream and season to taste. Serve immediately garnished with thyme and radicchio leaves.

Fish Stew with Calvados, Parsley and Dill

This rustic stew harbours all sorts of interesting flavours and will please and intrigue.
Many varieties of fish can be used, just choose the freshest and best.

INGREDIENTS

1 kg / 2 lb assorted white fish
1 tbsp chopped parsley, plus a few
leaves to garnish
225 g / 8 oz mushrooms
225 g / 8 oz can of tomatoes
salt and pepper
2 tsp flour
15 g / ½ oz / 1 tbsp butter
450 ml / ¾ pint cider
45 ml / 3 tbsp Calvados
1 large bunch fresh dill sprigs,
reserving 4 fronds to garnish

Serves 4

1

Chop the fish roughly and place it in a casserole or stewing pot with the parsley, mushrooms and tomatoes, adding salt and pepper to taste.

2

Preheat the oven to 180°C/350°F/Gas Mark 4. Work the flour into the butter. Heat the cider and stir in the flour and butter mixture a little at a time. Cook, stirring, until it has thickened slightly.

3

Add the cider mixture and the remaining ingredients to the fish and mix gently. Cover and bake for about 30 minutes. Serve garnished with sprigs of dill and parsley leaves.

Lamb and Leeks with Mint and Spring Onions

*If you do not have any home-made chicken stock, use a good
quality ready-made stock rather than a stock cube.*

INGREDIENTS

2 tbsp sunflower oil
2 kg / 4 lb lamb (fillet or boned leg)
10 spring onions, thickly sliced
3 leeks, thickly sliced
1 tbsp flour
150 ml / ¼ pint white wine
300 ml / ½ pint chicken stock
1 tbsp tomato purée
1 tbsp sugar
salt and pepper
2 tbsp fresh mint leaves, finely
chopped, plus a few more to garnish
115 g / 4 oz dried pears
1 kg / 2 lb potatoes, peeled and sliced
30 g / 1¼ oz melted butter

Serves 6

1

Heat the oil and fry the cubed lamb to seal
it. Transfer to a casserole. Preheat the oven
to 180°C/350°F/Gas Mark 4.

2

Fry the onions and leeks for 1 minute, stir
in the flour and cook for another minute.
Add the wine and stock and bring to the
boil. Add the tomato purée, sugar, salt and
pepper with the mint and chopped pears
and pour into the casserole. Stir the
mixture. Arrange the sliced potatoes on top
and brush with the melted butter.

3

Cover and bake for 1½ hours. Then
increase the temperature to 200°C/400°F/
Gas Mark 6, cook for a further 30 minutes,
uncovered, to brown the potatoes.
Garnish with mint leaves.

Stuffed Parsleyed Onions

Although devised as a vegetarian dish, these stuffed onions make a wonderful accompaniment to meat dishes, or an appetizing supper dish with crusty bread and a salad.

INGREDIENTS

4 large onions
4 tbsp cooked rice
4 tsp finely chopped fresh parsley,
plus extra to garnish
4 tbsp strong Cheddar cheese, finely
grated
salt and pepper
2 tbsp olive oil
1 tbsp white wine, to moisten

Serves 4

1

Cut a slice from the top of each onion and scoop out the centre to leave a thick shell.

2

Combine all the remaining ingredients, moistening with enough wine to mix well. Preheat the oven to 180°C/350°F/ Gas Mark 4.

3

Fill the onions and bake in the oven for 45 minutes. Serve garnished with parsley.

Spring Roasted Chicken with Fresh Herbs and Garlic

A smaller chicken or four poussins can also be roasted in this way.

INGREDIENTS

*1.75 kg / 4½ lb free-range chicken
or 4 small poussins
finely grated rind and
juice of 1 lemon
1 garlic clove, crushed
30 ml / 2 tbsp olive oil
2 fresh thyme sprigs
2 fresh sage sprigs
75 g / 3 oz / 6 tbsp unsalted butter,
softened
salt and freshly ground
black pepper*

Serves 4

1

Season the chicken or poussins well.
Mix the lemon rind and juice, garlic and
olive oil together and pour them over the
chicken. Leave to marinate for at least
2 hours in a non-metallic dish.
When the chicken has marinated preheat
the oven to 230°C / 450°F / Gas Mark 8.

2

Place the herbs in the cavity of the bird and
smear the butter over the skin. Season well.
Roast the chicken for 10 minutes, then turn
the oven down to 190°C / 375°F / Gas Mark 5.
Baste the chicken well, and then roast for a
further 1 hour 30 minutes, until the juices run
clear when the thigh is pierced with a skewer.
Leave to rest for 15 minutes before carving.

Lemon and Rosemary Lamb Chops

*Spring lamb is delicious with the fresh flavour of lemon. Garnish with sprigs of
fresh rosemary – the aroma is irresistible.*

INGREDIENTS

*12 lamb cutlets
45 ml / 3 tbsp olive oil
2 large rosemary sprigs
juice of 1 lemon
3 garlic cloves, sliced
salt and freshly ground
black pepper*

Serves 4

1

Trim the excess fat from the cutlets.
Mix the oil, rosemary, lemon juice and
garlic together and season well.

2

Pour over the chops in a shallow dish and
marinate for 30 minutes. Remove from the
marinade, and blot the excess with kitchen
paper and grill for 10 minutes on each side.

Carrot and Coriander Soufflés

Use tender young carrots for this light-as-air dish.

INGREDIENTS

450 g / 1 lb carrots
30 ml / 2 tbsp fresh chopped
coriander
4 eggs, separated
salt and freshly ground
black pepper

Serves 4

1

Peel the carrots.

2

Cook in boiling salted water for 20 minutes or until tender. Drain, and process until smooth in a food processor.

3

Preheat the oven to 200°C / 400°F / Gas Mark 6. Season the puréed carrots well, and stir in the chopped coriander.

4

Fold the egg yolks into the carrot mixture.

5

In a separate bowl, whisk the egg whites until stiff.

6

Fold the egg whites into the carrot mixture and pour into four greased ramekins. Bake for about 20 minutes or until risen and golden. Serve immediately.

Leeks with Ham and Cheese Sauce

A tasty teatime or supper dish: use a strong cheese for best results.

INGREDIENTS

4 leeks
4 slices ham

For the sauce
25 g / 1 oz / 2 tbsp unsalted butter
25 g / 1 oz / 1 tbsp plain flour
300 ml / ½ pint / 1¼ cups milk
½ tsp French mustard
115 g / 4 oz hard cheese, grated
salt and freshly ground
black pepper

Serves 4

1

Preheat the oven to 190°C / 375°F /
Gas Mark 5. Trim the leeks to 2 cm / 1 in of
the white and cook in salted water for about
20 minutes until soft. Drain thoroughly.
Wrap the leeks in the ham slices.

2

To make the sauce, melt the butter in a
saucepan. Add the flour and cook for a few
minutes. Remove from the heat and
gradually add the milk, whisking well with
each addition. Return to the heat and whisk
until the sauce thickens. Stir in the mustard
and 75 g / 3 oz of the cheese and season well.
Lay the leeks in a shallow ovenproof dish and
pour over the sauce. Scatter the extra cheese
on top and bake for 20 minutes.

Baked Eggs with Double Cream and Chives

This is a rich dish best served with Melba toast: it's very easy and quick to make.

INGREDIENTS

15 g / ½ oz / 1 tbsp unsalted
butter, softened
60 ml / 4 tbsp double cream
15 ml / 1 tbsp snipped fresh chives
4 eggs
50 g / 2 oz Gruyère cheese,
finely grated
salt and freshly ground
black pepper

Serves 2

1

Preheat the oven to 180°C / 350°F /
Gas Mark 4. Grease two individual gratin
dishes. Mix the cream with the chives,
and season with salt and pepper.

2

Break the eggs into each dish and top with
the cream mixture. Sprinkle the cheese
around the edges of the dishes and bake in
the oven for 15–20 minutes. When cooked,
brown the tops under the grill for a minute.

Lemon Drizzle Cake

*You can also make this recipe using a large orange instead of the lemons;
either way, it makes a zesty treat for afternoon tea.*

INGREDIENTS

finely grated rind of 2 lemons
175 g / 6 oz / 12 tbsp caster sugar
*225 g / 8 oz / 1 cup unsalted
butter, softened*
4 eggs
*225 g / 8 oz / 2 cups self-raising
flour*
5 ml / 1 tsp baking powder
¼ tsp salt
*shredded rind of 1 lemon,
to decorate*

For the syrup
juice of 1 lemon
150 g / 5 oz / ¾ cup caster sugar

Serves 6

1

Preheat the oven to 160°C / 325°F /
Gas Mark 3. Grease a 1 kg / 2 lb loaf tin or
18–20 cm / 7–8 in round cake tin and line it
with greaseproof paper or baking parchment.
Mix the lemon rind and caster sugar together.

2

Cream the butter with the lemon and sugar
mixture. Add the eggs and mix until
smooth. Sift the flour, baking powder and
salt into a bowl and fold a third at a time into
the mixture. Turn the batter into the tin,
smooth the top and bake for 1½ hours or
until golden brown and springy to the touch.

3

To make the syrup, slowly heat the juice
with the sugar and dissolve it gently. Make
several slashes in the top of the cake and pour
over the syrup. Sprinkle the shredded lemon
rind and 5 ml / 1 tsp granulated sugar on top
and leave to cool.

Wholemeal Bread

Home-made bread creates one of the most evocative smells in country cooking.
Eat this on the day of making, to enjoy the superb fresh taste.

INGREDIENTS

20 g / ¾ oz fresh yeast
300 ml / ½ pint / 1¼ cups
lukewarm milk
5 ml / 1 tsp caster sugar
225 g / 8 oz / 1½ cups strong
wholemeal flour, sifted
225 g / 8 oz / 2 cups strong
white flour, sifted
5 ml / 1 tsp salt
50 g / 2 oz / 4 tbsp butter,
chilled and cubed
1 egg, lightly beaten
30 ml / 2 tbsp mixed seeds

Makes 4 rounds or 2 loaves

1

Gently dissolve the yeast with a little of the milk and the sugar to make a paste. Place both the flours plus any bran from the sieve and the salt in a large warmed mixing bowl. Rub in the butter until the mixture resembles breadcrumbs.

2

Add the yeast mixture, remaining milk and egg and mix into a fairly soft dough. Knead on a floured board for 15 minutes. Lightly grease the mixing bowl and put the dough back in the bowl, covering it with a piece of greased cling film. Leave to double in size in a warm place (this should take at least an hour).

3

Knock the dough back and knead it for a further 10 minutes. Preheat the oven to 200°C / 400°F / Gas Mark 6. To make round loaves, divide the dough into four pieces and shape them into flattish rounds. Place them on a floured baking sheet and leave to rise for a further 15 minutes. Sprinkle the loaves with the mixed seeds. Bake for about 20 minutes until golden and firm.

NOTE

For tin-shaped loaves, put the knocked-back dough into two greased loaf tins instead. Leave to rise for a further 45 minutes and then bake for about 45 minutes, until the loaf sounds hollow when turned out of the tin and knocked on the base.

Rhubarb and Orange Crumble

The almonds give this crumble topping a nutty taste and crunchy texture.
This crumble is extra-delicious with home-made custard.

<u>INGREDIENTS</u>

900 g / 2 lb rhubarb, cut in
5 cm / 2 in lengths
75 g / 3 oz / 6 tbsp caster sugar
finely grated rind and juice
of 2 oranges

115 g / 4 oz / 1 cup plain flour
115 g / 4 oz / ½ cup unsalted
butter, chilled and cubed
75 g / 3 oz / 6 tbsp demerara sugar
115 g / 4 oz / 1¼ cups ground almonds

Serves 6

<u>1</u>

Preheat the oven to 180°C / 350°F /
Gas Mark 4. Place the rhubarb in a shallow
ovenproof dish.

<u>2</u>

Sprinkle over the caster sugar and add the
orange rind and juice.

<u>3</u>

Sift the flour into a mixing bowl and add the
butter. Rub the butter into the flour until
the mixture resembles breadcrumbs.

<u>4</u>

Add the demerara sugar and ground almonds
and mix well.

<u>5</u>

Spoon the crumble mixture over the fruit to
cover it completely. Bake for 40 minutes,
until the top is browned and the fruit is
cooked. Serve warm.

Summer Recipes

....

The warm, lazy days and light evenings of summer
provide the perfect excuse for outdoor dining
with friends and family. Try Mediterranean quiche
or a glorious French bean salad. Cooling treats
include strawberry fool, or homemade
mint ice cream.

Herb and Chilli Gazpacho

Gazpacho is a lovely soup, set off perfectly by the addition of a few herbs.

INGREDIENTS

1.2 kg / 2½ lb ripe tomatoes
225 g / 8 oz onions
2 green peppers
1 green chilli
1 large cucumber
30 ml / 2 tbsp red wine vinegar
15 ml / 1 tbsp balsamic vinegar
30 ml / 2 tbsp olive oil
1 clove of garlic, peeled and crushed
300 ml / ½ pint tomato juice
30 ml / 2 tbsp tomato purée
salt and pepper
2 tbsp finely chopped mixed fresh
herbs, plus some extra to garnish

Serves 6

1

Keep back about a quarter of all the fresh vegetables, except the green chilli, and place all the remaining ingredients in a food processor and season to taste. Process finely and chill in the refrigerator.

2

Chop all the remaining vegetables and serve in a separate bowl to sprinkle over the soup. Crush some ice cubes and add to the centre of each bowl and garnish with fresh herbs. Serve with bread rolls.

Pear and Watercress Soup with Stilton Croûtons

*Pears and Stilton taste very good when you eat them together after the main course –
here, for a change, they are served as a starter.*

INGREDIENTS

*1 bunch watercress
4 medium pears, sliced
900 ml / 1½ pints chicken stock,
preferably home-made
salt and pepper
120 ml / 4 fl oz double cream
juice of 1 lime*

*For the croûtons
25g / 1oz butter
30 ml / 1 tbsp olive oil
200 g / 7 oz cubed stale bread
140 g / 5 oz chopped Stilton cheese*

Serves 6

1

Keep back about a third of the watercress
leaves. Place all the rest of the watercress
leaves and stalks in a pan with the pears,
stock and a little seasoning. Simmer for
about 15–20 minutes.

2

Reserving some watercress leaves for
garnishing, add the rest of the leaves and
immediately blend in a food processor until
smooth.

3

Put the mixture into a bowl and stir in the
cream and lime juice to mix the flavours
thoroughly. Season again to taste. Pour all
the soup back into a pan and reheat,
stirring gently until warmed through.

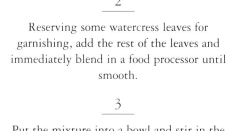

4

To make the croûtons, melt the butter and
oil and fry the bread cubes until golden
brown. Drain on kitchen paper. Put the
cheese on top and heat under a hot grill
until bubbling. Reheat the soup and pour
into bowls. Divide the croûtons and
remaining watercress between the bowls.

Mackerel with Roasted Blueberries

Fresh blueberries burst with flavour when roasted, and their sharpness complements the rich flesh of mackerel very well.

INGREDIENTS

15 g / ½ oz / 2 tsp plain flour
4 small cooked, smoked mackerel fillets
50 g / 2 oz / 4 tbsp unsalted butter
juice of ½ lemon
salt and freshly ground black pepper

For the roasted blueberries
450 g / 1 lb blueberries
25 g / 1 oz / 2 tbsp caster sugar
15 g / ½ oz / 1 tbsp unsalted butter
salt and freshly ground black pepper

Serves 4

1

Preheat the oven to 200°C / 400°F / Gas Mark 6. Season the flour. Dip each fish fillet into the flour to coat it well.

2

Dot the butter on the fillets and bake in the oven for 20 minutes.

3

Place the blueberries, sugar, butter and seasoning in a separate small roasting tin and roast them, basting them occasionally, for 15 minutes. To serve, drizzle the lemon juice over the roasted mackerel, accompanied by the roasted blueberries.

Griddled Trout with Bacon

This dish can also be cooked on the barbecue.

INGREDIENTS

25 g / 1 oz / 1 tbsp plain flour
4 trout, cleaned and gutted
75 g / 3 oz streaky bacon
50 g / 2 oz / 4 tbsp butter
15 ml / 1 tbsp olive oil
juice of ½ lemon
salt and freshly ground
black pepper

Serves 4

1

Pat the trout dry with kitchen roll and
mix the flour and seasoning together.

2

Roll the trout in the seasoned flour mixture
and wrap tightly in the streaky bacon.
Heat a heavy frying pan. Heat the butter and
oil in the pan and fry the trout for 5 minutes
on each side. Serve immediately, with the
lemon juice drizzled on top.

Cod, Basil and Tomato with a Potato Thatch

With a green salad, this makes an ideal dish for lunch or a family supper.

INGREDIENTS

1 kg / 2 lb smoked cod
1 kg / 2 lb white cod
600 ml / 1 pint milk
2 sprigs basil
1 sprig lemon thyme
75 g / 3 oz butter
1 onion, peeled and chopped
75 g / 3 oz flour
30 ml / 2 tbsp tomato purée
2 tbsp chopped basil
12 medium-sized old potatoes
50 g / 2 oz butter
300 ml / ½ pint milk
salt and pepper
1 tbsp chopped parsley

Serves 8

1

Place both kinds of fish in a roasting pan with the milk, 1.2 litres / 2 pints water and herbs. Simmer for about 3–4 minutes. Leave to cool in the liquid for about 20 minutes. Drain the fish, reserving the liquid for use in the sauce. Flake the fish, taking care to remove any skin and bone, which should be discarded.

2

Melt the butter in a pan, add the onion and cook for about 4 minutes until tender but not browned. Add the flour, tomato purée and half the basil. Gradually add the reserved fish stock, adding a little more milk if necessary to make a fairly thin sauce. Bring this to the boil, season with salt and pepper, and add the remaining basil. Add the fish carefully and stir gently. Pour into an ovenproof dish.

3

Preheat the oven to 180°C / 350°F / Gas Mark 4. Boil the potatoes until tender. Add the butter and milk, and mash well. Add salt and pepper to taste and cover the fish, forking to create a pattern. If you like, you can freeze the pie at this stage. Bake for 30 minutes. Serve with chopped parsley.

Lamb with Mint and Lemon

Lamb has been served with mint for many years – it is a great combination.

INGREDIENTS

8 lamb steaks, 225 g / 8 oz each
grated rind and juice of 1 lemon
2 cloves garlic, peeled and crushed
2 spring onions, finely chopped
2 tsp finely chopped fresh mint
leaves, plus some leaves for
garnishing
4 tbsp extra virgin olive oil
salt and black pepper

Serves 8

1

Make a marinade for the lamb by mixing all the other ingredients and seasoning to taste. Place the lamb steaks in a shallow dish and cover with the marinade. Refrigerate overnight.

2

Grill the lamb under a high heat until just cooked, basting with the marinade occasionally during cooking. Turn once during cooking. Serve garnished with fresh mint leaves.

Mediterranean Quiche

The strong Mediterranean flavours of tomatoes, peppers and anchovies complement beautifully the cheesy pastry in this unusual quiche.

INGREDIENTS

For the pastry
225 g / 8 oz / 2 cups plain flour
pinch of salt
pinch of dry mustard
115 g / 4 oz / ½ cup butter,
chilled and cubed
50 g / 2 oz Gruyère cheese, grated

For the filling
50 g / 2 oz can of anchovies in oil,
drained
50 ml / 2 fl oz / ¼ cup milk
30 ml / 2 tbsp French mustard
45 ml / 3 tbsp olive oil
2 large Spanish onions, sliced
1 red pepper, seeded and
very finely sliced
3 egg yolks
350 ml / 12 fl oz / 1½ cups
double cream
1 garlic clove, crushed
175 g / 6 oz mature Cheddar
cheese, grated
2 large tomatoes, thickly sliced
salt and freshly ground
black pepper
30 ml / 2 tbsp chopped fresh basil,
to garnish

Serves 12

1

First make the pastry. Place the flour, salt and mustard powder in a food processor, add the butter and process the mixture until it resembles breadcrumbs.

2

Add the cheese and process again briefly. Add enough iced water to make a stiff dough: it will be ready when the dough forms a ball. Wrap with cling film and chill for 30 minutes.

3

Meanwhile, make the filling. Soak the anchovies in the milk for 20 minutes. Drain away the milk.

4

Roll out the chilled pastry and line a 23 cm / 9 in loose-based flan tin. Spread over the mustard and chill for a further 15 minutes.

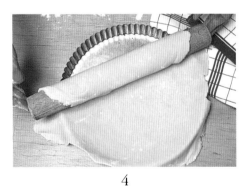

5

Preheat the oven to 200°C / 400°F / Gas Mark 6. Heat the oil in a frying pan and cook the onions and red pepper until soft. In a separate bowl, beat the egg yolks, cream, garlic and Cheddar cheese together; season well. Arrange the tomatoes in a single layer in the pastry case. Top with the onion and pepper mixture and the anchovy fillets. Pour over the egg mixture. Bake for 30–35 minutes. Sprinkle over the basil and serve.

New Potato Salad

Potatoes freshly dug up from the garden are the best. Always leave the skins on:
just wash the dirt away thoroughly. If you add the mayonnaise and other
ingredients when the potatoes are hot, the flavours will develop as the potatoes cool.

INGREDIENTS

900 g / 2 lb baby new potatoes
2 green apples, cored and chopped
4 spring onions, chopped
3 celery sticks, finely chopped
150 ml / ¼ pint / ⅔ cup
mayonnaise
salt and freshly ground
black pepper

Serves 6

1

Cook the potatoes in salted, boiling water for about 20 minutes, or until they are very tender.

2

Drain the potatoes well and immediately add the remaining ingredients and stir until well mixed. Leave to cool and serve cold.

French Bean Salad

The secret of this recipe is to dress the beans while still hot.

INGREDIENTS

175 g / 6 oz cherry tomatoes,
halved
5 ml / 1 tsp sugar
450 g / 1 lb French beans,
topped and tailed
175 g / 6 oz feta cheese, cubed
salt and freshly ground
black pepper

For the dressing
90 ml / 6 tbsp olive oil
45 ml / 3 tbsp white-wine vinegar
¼ tsp Dijon mustard
2 garlic cloves, crushed
salt and freshly ground
black pepper

Serves 6

1

Preheat the oven to 230°C / 450°F / Gas Mark 8. Put the cherry tomatoes on a baking sheet and sprinkle over the sugar, salt and pepper. Roast for 20 minutes, then leave to cool. Meanwhile, cook the beans in boiling, salted water for 10 minutes.

2

Make the dressing by whisking together the oil, vinegar, mustard, garlic and seasoning. Drain the beans and immediately pour over the vinaigrette and mix well. When cool, stir in the roasted tomatoes and the feta cheese. Serve chilled.

Smoked Salmon and Dill Pasta

This has been tried and tested as both a main-dish salad and a starter, and the only preference stated was that as a main dish you got a larger portion.

INGREDIENTS

salt
350 g / 12 oz pasta twists
6 large sprigs fresh dill, chopped,
plus more sprigs to garnish
30 ml / 2 tbsp extra virgin olive oil
15 ml / 1 tbsp white wine vinegar
300 ml / ½ pint double cream
pepper
170 g / 6 oz smoked salmon

Serves 2 as a main course

1

Boil the pasta in salted water until it is just cooked. Drain and run under the cold tap until completely cooled. Make the dressing by combining all the remaining ingredients, apart from the smoked salmon and reserved dill, in the bowl of a food processor and blend well. Season to taste.

2

Slice the salmon into small strips. Place the cooled pasta and the smoked salmon, in a mixing bowl. Pour on the dressing and toss carefully. Transfer to a serving bowl and garnish with the dill sprigs.

Avocado and Pasta Salad with Coriander

Served as one of a variety of salads or alone, this tasty combination is sure to please.

INGREDIENTS

115 g / 4 oz pasta shells or bows
900 ml / 1½ pints chicken stock
4 sticks celery, finely chopped
2 avocados, chopped
1 clove garlic, peeled and chopped
1 tbsp finely chopped fresh coriander,
plus some whole leaves to garnish
115 g / 4 oz grated mature
Cheddar cheese

For the dressing
150 ml / ¼ pint extra virgin olive oil
15 ml / 1 tbsp cider vinegar
30 ml / 2 tbsp lemon juice
grated rind of 1 lemon
5 ml / 1 tsp French mustard
1 tbsp chopped fresh coriander
salt and pepper

Serves 4

1

Bring the chicken stock to the boil, add the pasta, and simmer for about 10 minutes until just cooked. Drain and cool under cold running water.

2

Mix the celery, avocados, garlic and chopped coriander in a bowl and add the cooled pasta. Sprinkle with the grated Cheddar.

3

Place all the ingredients for the dressing in a food processor and mix until the coriander is finely chopped. Serve separately or pour over the salad and toss before serving. Garnish with coriander leaves.

Country Strawberry Fool

*Make this delicious fool on the day you want to eat it, and chill it well,
for the best strawberry taste.*

INGREDIENTS

300 ml / ½ pint / 1¼ cups milk
2 egg yolks
*90 g / 3½ oz / scant ½ cup
caster sugar*
few drops of vanilla essence
900 g / 2 lb ripe strawberries
juice of ½ lemon
*300 ml / ½ pint / 1¼ cups double
cream*

To decorate
12 small strawberries
4 fresh mint sprigs

Serves 4

1

First make the custard. Whisk 30 ml / 2 tbsp
milk with the egg yolks, 15 ml / 1 tbsp caster
sugar and the vanilla essence.

2

Heat the remaining milk until it is just
below boiling point.

3

Stir the milk into the egg mixture. Rinse
the pan out and return the mixture to it.

4

Gently heat and whisk until the mixture
thickens (it should be thick enough to coat
the back of a spoon). Lay a wet piece of
greaseproof paper on top of the custard and
leave it to cool.

5

Purée the strawberries in a food processor or
blender with the lemon juice and the
remaining sugar.

6

Lightly whip the cream and fold in the fruit
purée and custard. Pour into glass dishes and
decorate with the whole strawberries and
sprigs of mint.

Mint Ice Cream

*This ice cream is best served slightly softened, so take it out
of the freezer 20 minutes before you want to serve it. For a special occasion,
this looks spectacular served in an ice bowl.*

INGREDIENTS

*8 egg yolks
75 g / 3 oz / 6 tbsp caster sugar
600 ml / 1 pint / 2½ cups single
cream
1 vanilla pod
60 ml / 4 tbsp chopped fresh mint*

Serves 8

1

Beat the egg yolks and sugar until they are
pale and light using a hand-held electric
beater or a balloon whisk. Transfer to a
small saucepan.

2

In a separate saucepan, bring the cream to
the boil with the vanilla pod.

3

Remove the vanilla pod and pour the hot cream
on to the egg mixture, whisking briskly.

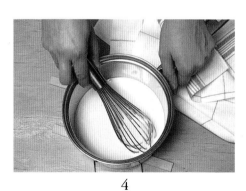

4

Continue whisking to ensure the eggs
are mixed into the cream.

5

Gently heat the mixture until the custard
thickens enough to coat the back of a
wooden spoon. Leave to cool.

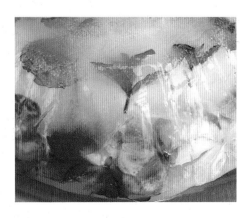

6

Stir in the mint and place in an ice-cream
maker to churn, about 3–4 hours. If you
don't have an ice-cream maker, freeze the
ice cream until mushy and then whisk it well
again, to break down the ice crystals. Freeze
for another 3 hours until it is softly frozen
and whisk again. Finally freeze until hard:
at least 6 hours.

Mixed Berry Tart

The orange-flavoured pastry is delicious with the fresh fruits of summer.
Serve this with some extra shreds of orange rind scattered on top.

INGREDIENTS

For the pastry
225 g / 8 oz / 2 cups plain flour
115 g / 4 oz / ½ cup unsalted
butter
finely grated rind of 1 orange,
plus extra to decorate

For the filling
300 ml / ½ pint / 1¼ cups
crème fraîche
finely grated rind of 1 lemon
10 ml / 2 tsp icing sugar
675 g / 1½ lb mixed
summer berries

Serves 8

1

To make the pastry, put the flour and butter in a large bowl. Rub in the butter until the mixture resembles breadcrumbs.

2

Add the orange rind and enough cold water to make a soft dough.

3

Roll into a ball and chill for at least 30 minutes. Roll out the pastry on a lightly floured surface.

4

Line a 23 cm / 9 in loose-based flan tin with the pastry. Chill for 30 minutes. Preheat the oven to 200°C / 400°F / Gas Mark 6 and place a baking sheet in the oven to heat up. Line the tin with greaseproof paper and baking beans and bake blind on the baking sheet for 15 minutes. Remove the paper and beans and bake for 10 minutes more, until the pastry is golden. Allow to cool completely. To make the filling, whisk the crème fraîche, lemon rind and sugar together and pour into the pastry case. Top with fruit, sprinkle with orange rind and serve sliced.

Autumn Recipes

Reap the benefits of the autumn harvest with this collection of recipes; wild mushroom tart, thyme-roasted onions and chicken with sloe gin and juniper all make the most of autumn produce. Warming desserts such as blackberry charlotte and apple tart are guaranteed to keep away the autumn chill.

Wild Mushroom Tart

The flavour of wild mushrooms makes this tart really rich: use as wide a variety
of mushrooms as you can get.

<u>INGREDIENTS</u>

For the pastry
225 g / 8 oz / 2 cups plain flour
50 g / 2 oz / 4 tbsp hard white fat
10 ml / 2 tsp lemon juice
about 150 ml / ¼ pint / ⅔ cup
ice-cold water
115 g / 4 oz / ½ cup butter,
chilled and cubed
1 egg, beaten, to glaze

For the filling
150 g / 5 oz / 10 tbsp butter
2 shallots, finely chopped
2 garlic cloves, crushed
450 g / 1 lb mixed wild
mushrooms, sliced
45 ml / 3 tbsp chopped fresh parsley
30 ml / 2 tbsp double cream
salt and freshly ground
black pepper

Serves 6

<u>1</u>

To make the pastry, sieve the flour and
½ tsp salt together into a large bowl.
Add the white fat and rub into the mixture
until it resembles breadcrumbs.

<u>2</u>

Add the lemon juice and enough iced water
to make a soft but not sticky dough.
Cover and chill for 20 minutes.

<u>3</u>

Roll the pastry out into a rectangle on a
lightly floured surface. Mark the dough into
three equal strips and arrange half the butter
cubes over two-thirds of the dough.

<u>5</u>

Chill the pastry for 20 minutes. Repeat the
process of marking into thirds, folding over,
giving a quarter turn and rolling out three
times, chilling for 20 minutes in between
each time. To make the filling, melt
50 g / 2 oz / 4 tbsp butter and fry the shallots
and garlic until soft but not browned. Add
the remaining butter and the mushrooms
and cook for 35–40 minutes. Drain off any
excess liquid and stir in the remaining
ingredients. Leave to cool. Preheat the oven
to 220°C / 450°F / Gas Mark 7.

<u>4</u>

Fold the outer two-thirds over, folding over
the uncovered third last. Seal the edges with
a rolling pin. Give the dough a quarter turn
and roll it out again. Mark it into thirds and
dot with the remaining butter cubes
in the same way.

<u>6</u>

Divide the pastry in two. Roll out one half
into a 22 cm / 9 in round, cutting around a
plate to make a neat shape. Pile the filling
into the centre. Roll out the remaining
pastry large enough to cover the base. Brush
the edges of the base with water and then lay
the second pastry circle on top. Press the
edges together to seal and brush the top with
a little beaten egg. Bake for 45 minutes,
or until the pastry is risen, golden and flaky.

Mushroom and Parsley Soup

Thickened with bread, this rich mushroom soup will warm you up on cold autumn days. It makes a terrific hearty lunch.

INGREDIENTS

75 g / 3 oz / 6 tbsp unsalted butter
900 g / 2 lb field mushrooms,
sliced
2 onions, roughly chopped
600 ml / 1 pint / 2½ cups milk
8 slices white bread
60 ml / 4 tbsp chopped fresh parsley
300 ml / ½ pint / 1¼ cups
double cream
salt and freshly ground
black pepper

Serves 8

1

Melt the butter and sauté the mushrooms
and onions until soft but not coloured –
about 10 minutes. Add the milk.

2

Tear the bread into pieces, drop them into
the soup and leave the bread to soak for
15 minutes. Purée the soup and return it to
the pan. Add the parsley, cream and seasoning.
Re-heat, but do not allow the soup to boil.
Serve at once.

Thyme-roasted Onions

These slowly roasted onions develop a delicious, sweet flavour which is perfect with roast meat. You could prepare par-boiled new potatoes in the same way.

INGREDIENTS

75 ml / 5 tbsp olive oil
50 g / 2 oz / 4 tbsp unsalted butter
900 g / 2 lb small onions
30 ml / 2 tbsp chopped fresh thyme
salt and freshly ground
black pepper

Serves 4

1

Preheat the oven to 220°C / 425°F /
Gas Mark 7. Heat the oil and butter in a
large roasting tin. Add the onions and toss
them in the oil and butter mixture.

2

Add the thyme and seasoning and roast for
45 minutes, basting regularly.

Spinach, Cognac, Garlic and Chicken Pâté

INGREDIENTS

12 slices streaky bacon
2 tbsp butter
1 onion, peeled and chopped
1 clove garlic, peeled and crushed
285 g / 10 oz frozen spinach, thawed
50 g / 2 oz wholemeal breadcrumbs
30 ml / 2 tbsp Cognac
500 g / 1 lb minced chicken
(dark and light meat)
500 g / 1 lb minced pork
2 eggs, beaten
2 tbsp chopped mixed fresh herbs,
such as parsley, sage and dill
salt and pepper

Serves 12

1

Fry the bacon in a pan until it is only just done, then arrange it round the sides of a 900 ml / 1½ pints dish, if possible leaving a couple of slices to garnish.

3

Preheat the oven to 180°C / 350°F / Gas Mark 4. Combine all the remaining ingredients, apart from any remaining bacon strips, in a bowl and mix well to blend. Spoon the pâté into the loaf tin and cover with any remaining bacon.

2

Melt the butter in a pan. Fry the onion and garlic until soft. Squeeze the spinach to remove as much water as possible, then add to the pan, stirring until the spinach is dry.

4

Cover the tin with a double thickness of foil and set it in a baking pan. Pour 2.5 cm / 1 in boiling water into the baking pan. Bake for about 1¼ hours. Remove the pâté and let it cool. Place a heavy weight on top of the pâté and refrigerate overnight.

Beef, Celeriac and Horseradish Pâté

INGREDIENTS

500 g / 1 lb topside of beef, cubed
350 ml / 12 fl oz red wine
85 ml / 3 fl oz Madeira
250 ml / 8 fl oz beef or chicken stock
2 tbsp finely chopped celeriac
15 ml / 1 tbsp horseradish cream
salt and pepper
2 bay leaves
2 tbsp brandy
170 g / 6 oz butter, melted

Serves 4

1

Preheat the oven to 130°C / 250°F / Gas Mark ½. Place the beef in a casserole. Mix all the other ingredients together except the brandy and butter, and pour them over the beef. Cover tightly and cook for 2 hours.

3

Melt the remaining butter, skim any foam off the top and pour over the top of the beef, leaving any residue at the bottom of the pan. Cover the pâté and refrigerate overnight.

2

Remove and drain. Strain the liquid and reduce to about 45 ml / 3 tbsp. Slice and roughly chop the meat and put it with the reduced liquid in the food processor. Blend until fairly smooth. Add the brandy and a third of the butter. Turn into a pâté dish and leave to cool.

Chicken Stew with Blackberries and Lemon Balm

INGREDIENTS

4 chicken breasts, partly boned
salt and pepper
25 g / 1oz / scant 2 tbsp butter
15 ml / 1 tbsp sunflower oil
25 g / 1 oz / 4 tbsp flour
150 ml / ¼ pint/ / ⅔ cup red wine
150 ml / ¼ pint / ⅔ cup chicken stock
grated rind of half an orange plus
15 ml / 1 tbsp juice
3 sprigs lemon balm, finely chopped,
plus 1 sprig to garnish
150 ml / ¼ pint / ⅔ cup double cream
1 egg yolk
100 g / 4 oz / ⅔ cup fresh blackberries,
plus 50 g / 2 oz / ⅓ cup to garnish

Serves 4

1

Remove any skin from the chicken, and season the meat. Heat the butter and oil in a pan, fry the chicken to seal it, then transfer to a casserole dish. Stir the flour into the pan, then add wine and stock and bring to the boil. Add the orange rind and juice, and also the chopped lemon balm. Pour over the chicken.

2

Preheat the oven to 180°C/350°F/Gas Mark 4. Cover the casserole and cook in the oven for about 40 minutes.

3

Blend the cream with the egg yolk, add some of the liquid from the casserole and stir back into the dish with the blackberries (reserving those for the garnish). Cover and cook for another 10–15 minutes. Serve garnished with the rest of the blackberries and lemon balm.

Pork and Mushrooms with Sage and Mango Chutney

INGREDIENTS

25 g / 1 oz / scant 2 tbsp butter
1 tbsp sunflower oil
750 g / 1½ lb cubed pork
175 g / 6 oz onion, peeled and
chopped
2 tbsp flour
450 ml / ¾ pint / 1⅞ cups stock
60 ml / 4 tbsp white wine
salt and pepper
225 g / 8 oz mushrooms, sliced
6 fresh sage leaves, finely chopped
2 tbsp mango chutney
1 fresh mango, peeled and sliced, to
garnish

Serves 4

1

Heat the butter and oil and fry the pork in a pan to seal it. Transfer to a casserole. Fry the onion in the pan, stir in the flour and cook for 1 minute. Preheat the oven to 180°C/350°F/Gas Mark 4.

2

Gradually add the stock and white wine to the onion and bring to the boil. Season well and add the mushrooms, sage leaves and mango chutney. Pour the sauce mixture over the pork and cover the casserole. Cook in the oven for about 1 hour, depending on the cut of pork, until tender. Check the seasoning, garnish with mango slices, and serve with rice.

Chicken with Sloe Gin and Juniper

Juniper is used in the manufacture of gin, and this dish is flavoured with both
sloe gin and juniper. Sloe gin is easy to make and
has a wonderful flavour, but it can also be bought ready-made.

INGREDIENTS

2 tbsp butter
30 ml / 2 tbsp sunflower oil
8 chicken breast fillets, skinned
350 g / 12 oz carrots, cooked
1 clove garlic, peeled and crushed
1 tbsp finely chopped parsley
60 ml / 2 fl oz / ¼ cup chicken stock
60 ml / 2 fl oz / ¼ cup red wine
60 ml / 2 fl oz / ¼ cup sloe gin
1 tsp crushed juniper berries
salt and pepper
1 bunch basil, to garnish

Serves 8

1

Melt the butter with the oil in a pan, and sauté the chicken fillets until they are browned on all sides.

2

In a food processor, combine all the remaining ingredients except the basil, and blend to a smooth purée. If the mixture seems too thick add a little more red wine or water until a thinner consistency is reached.

3

Put the chicken breasts in a pan, pour the sauce over the top and cook until the chicken is cooked through, which should take about 15 minutes. Adjust the seasoning and serve garnished with chopped fresh basil leaves.

Spicy Duck Breasts with Red Plums

Duck breasts can be bought separately, which makes this dish very easy to prepare.

INGREDIENTS

*4 duck breasts, 175 g / 6 oz
each, skinned
salt
2 tsp stick cinnamon, crushed
50 g / 2 oz butter
1 tbsp plum brandy (or Cognac)
250 ml / 8 fl oz chicken stock
250 ml / 8 fl oz double cream
pepper
6 fresh red plums, stoned and sliced
6 sprigs coriander leaves, plus some
extra to garnish*

Serves 4

1

Preheat the oven to 190°C/375°F/Gas Mark 5. Score the duck breasts and sprinkle with salt. Press the crushed cinnamon on to both sides of the duck breasts. Melt half the butter in a pan and fry them on both sides to seal, then place in an ovenproof dish with the butter and bake for 6–7 minutes.

2

Remove the dish from the oven and return the contents to the pan. Add the brandy and set it alight. When the flames have died down, remove from the pan and keep warm. Add the stock and cream to the pan and simmer gently until reduced and thick. Adjust the seasoning.

3

Reserve a few plum slices for garnishing. In a pan, melt the other half of the butter and fry the plums and coriander, just enough to cook the fruit through. Slice the duck breasts and pour some sauce around each one, then garnish with slices of plum and chopped coriander.

Stuffed Tomatoes, with Wild Rice, Corn and Coriander

These tomatoes could be served as a light meal or as an accompaniment for meat or fish.

INGREDIENTS

8 medium tomatoes
50g / 2oz sweetcorn kernels
2 tbsp white wine
50g / 2oz cooked wild rice
1 clove garlic
50g / 2oz grated Cheddar cheese
1 tbsp chopped fresh coriander
salt and pepper
1 tbsp olive oil

Serves 4

1

Cut the tops off the tomatoes and remove the seeds with a small teaspoon. Scoop out all the flesh and chop finely – remember to chop the tops as well.

2

Preheat the oven to 180°C/350°F/Gas Mark 4. Put the chopped tomato in a pan. Add the sweetcorn and the white wine. Cover with a close-fitting lid and simmer until tender. Drain the excess liquid.

3

Mix together all the remaining ingredients except the olive oil, adding salt and pepper to taste. Carefully spoon the mixture into the tomatoes, piling it higher in the centre. Sprinkle the oil over the top, arrange the tomatoes in an ovenproof dish and bake at 180°C/350°F/Gas Mark 4 for 15–20 minutes until cooked through.

Spinach, Walnut and Gruyère Lasagne with Basil

This nutty lasagne is a delicious combination of flavours that easily equals the traditional meat and tomato version.

INGREDIENTS

*350 g / 12 oz spinach lasagne
(quick cooking)*

For the walnut and tomato sauce
*45 ml / 3 tbsp walnut oil
1 large onion, chopped
225 g / 8 oz celeriac, finely chopped
400g / 14oz can chopped tomatoes
1 large clove garlic, finely chopped
½ tsp sugar
115 g / 4 oz / ⅔ cup chopped walnuts
150 ml / ¼ pint / ⅔ cup Dubonnet*

For the spinach and Gruyère sauce
*75 g / 3 oz / ⅓ cup butter
30 ml / 2 tbsp walnut oil
1 medium onion, chopped
75 g / 3 oz / ⅔ cup flour
1 tsp mustard powder
1.2 litres / 2 pints / 5 cups milk
225 g / 8 oz / 2 cups grated
Gruyère cheese
salt and pepper
ground nutmeg
500 g / 1 lb frozen spinach, thawed
and puréed
2 tbsp basil, chopped*

Serves 8

1

First make the walnut and tomato sauce. Heat the walnut oil and sauté the onion and celeriac. Cook for about 8–10 minutes. Meanwhile purée the tomatoes in a food processor. Add the garlic to the pan and cook for about 1 minute, then add the sugar, walnuts, tomatoes and Dubonnet. Season to taste. Simmer, uncovered, for 25 minutes.

2

To make the spinach and Gruyère sauce, melt the butter with the walnut oil and add the onion. Cook for 5 minutes, then stir in the flour. Cook for another minute and add the mustard powder and milk, stirring vigorously. When the sauce has come to the boil, take off the heat and add three-quarters of the grated Gruyère. Season to taste with salt, pepper and nutmeg. Finally add the puréed spinach.

3

Preheat the oven to 180°C/350°F/Gas Mark 4. Layer the lasagne in an ovenproof dish. Start with a layer of the spinach and Gruyère sauce, then add a little walnut and tomato sauce, then a layer of lasagne, and continue until the dish is full, ending with a layer of either sauce. Sprinkle the remaining Gruyère over the top of the dish, followed by the basil. Bake for 45 minutes.

Cheese Scones

These delicious scones make a good tea-time treat. They are best served fresh and still slightly warm.

INGREDIENTS

225 g / 8 oz / 2 cups plain flour
12 ml / 2 ½ tsp baking powder
½ tsp dry mustard powder
½ tsp salt
50 g / 2 oz / 4 tbsp butter, chilled
75 g / 3 oz Cheddar cheese, grated
150 ml / ¼ pint / ⅔ cup milk
1 egg, beaten

Makes 12

1

Preheat the oven to 230°C / 450°F / Gas Mark 8. Sift the flour, baking powder, mustard powder and salt into a mixing bowl. Add the butter and rub it into the flour mixture until the mixture resembles breadcrumbs. Stir in 50 g / 2 oz of the cheese.

2

Make a well in the centre and add the milk and egg. Mix gently and then turn the dough out on to a lightly floured surface. Roll it out and cut it into triangles or squares. Brush lightly with milk and sprinkle with the remaining cheese. Leave to rest for 15 minutes, then bake them for 15 minutes, or until well risen.

Oatcakes

These are very simple to make and are an excellent addition to a cheese board.

INGREDIENTS

225 g / 8 oz / 1 ⅔ cups medium oatmeal
75 g / 3 oz / ¾ cup plain flour
¼ tsp bicarbonate of soda
5 ml / 1 tsp salt
25 g / 1 oz / 2 tbsp hard white vegetable fat
25 g / 1 oz / 2 tbsp butter

Makes 24

1

Preheat the oven to 220°C / 425°F / Gas Mark 7. Place the oatmeal, flour, soda and salt in a large bowl. Gently melt the two fats together in a pan.

2

Add the melted fat and enough boiling water to make a soft dough. Turn out on to a surface scattered with a little oatmeal. Roll out the dough thinly and cut it into circles. Bake the oatcakes on ungreased baking trays for 15 minutes, until crisp.

Blackberry Charlotte

A classic pudding, perfect for cold days. Serve with lightly whipped cream or home-made custard.

INGREDIENTS

65 g / 2½ oz / 5 tbsp unsalted butter
175 g / 6 oz / 3 cups fresh white breadcrumbs
50 g / 2 oz / 4 tbsp soft brown sugar
60 ml / 4 tbsp golden syrup
finely grated rind and juice of 2 lemons
50 g / 2 oz walnut halves
450 g / 1 lb blackberries
450 g / 1 lb cooking apples, peeled, cored and finely sliced

Serves 4

1

Preheat the oven to 180°C / 350°F / Gas Mark 4. Grease a 450 ml / ¾ pint / 2 cup dish with 15 g / ½ oz / 1 tbsp of the butter. Melt the remaining butter and add the breadcrumbs. Sauté them for 5–7 minutes, until the crumbs are a little crisp and golden. Leave to cool slightly.

2

Place the sugar, syrup, lemon rind and juice in a small saucepan and gently warm them. Add the crumbs.

3

Process the walnuts until they are finely ground.

4

Arrange a thin layer of blackberries on the dish. Top with a thin layer of crumbs.

5

Add a thin layer of apple, topping it with another thin layer of crumbs. Repeat the process with another layer of blackberries, followed by a layer of crumbs. Continue until you have used up all the ingredients, finishing with a layer of crumbs. The mixture should be piled well above the top edge of the dish, because it shrinks during cooking. Bake for 30 minutes, until the crumbs are golden and the fruit is soft.

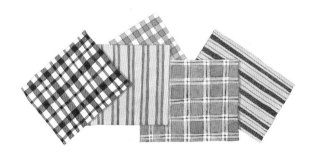

French Apple Tart

For added flavour, scatter some toasted, flaked almonds over the top of this classic tart.

INGREDIENTS

For the pastry
*115 g / 4 oz / ½ cup unsalted
butter, softened
50 g / 2 oz / 4 tbsp vanilla sugar
1 egg
225 g / 8 oz / 2 cups plain flour*

For the filling
*50 g / 2 oz / 4 tbsp unsalted butter
5 large tart apples, peeled, cored
and sliced
juice of ½ lemon
300 ml / ½ pint / 1¼ cups double
cream
2 egg yolks
25 g / 1 oz / 2 tbsp vanilla sugar
50 g / 2 oz / ⅔ cup ground
almonds, toasted
25 g / 1 oz / 2 tbsp flaked almonds,
toasted, to garnish*

Serves 8

1

Place the butter and sugar in a food processor and process them well together. Add the egg and process to mix it in well.

2

Add the flour and process till you have a soft dough. Wrap the dough in cling film and chill it for 30 minutes.

3

Roll the pastry out on a lightly floured surface to about 22–25 cm / 9–10 in diameter.

4

Line a flan tin with the pastry and chill it for a further 30 minutes. Preheat the oven to 220°C / 425°F / Gas Mark 7 and place a baking sheet in the oven to heat up. Line the pastry case with greaseproof paper and baking beans and bake blind on the baking sheet for 10 minutes. Then remove the beans and paper and cook for a further 5 minutes.

5

Turn the oven down to 190°C / 375°F / Gas Mark 5. To make the filling, melt the butter in a frying pan and lightly sauté the apples for 5–7 minutes. Sprinkle the apples with lemon juice.

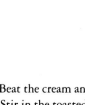

6

Beat the cream and egg yolks with the sugar. Stir in the toasted ground almonds. Arrange the apple slices on top of the warm pastry and pour over the cream mixture. Bake for 25 minutes, or until the cream is just about set – it tastes better if the cream is still slightly runny in the centre. Serve hot or cold, scattered with flaked almonds.

Winter Recipes

With the nights drawing in, we all need something
substantial and warming to keep out the cold.
Try roast beef with roasted peppers, or raised
country pie. Scotch pancakes or cranberry muffins
are a perfect fire-side treat, and rich Christmas
pudding is the perfect way to round off the year.

Roast Beef with Porcini and Roasted Sweet Peppers

A substantial and warming dish for cold, dark evenings.

INGREDIENTS

1.5 kg / 3–3½ lb piece of sirloin
15 ml / 1 tbsp olive oil
450 g / 1 lb small red peppers
115 g / 4 oz mushrooms
175 g / 6 oz thick-sliced pancetta
or smoked bacon, cubed
50 g / 2 oz / 2 tbsp plain flour
150 ml / ¼ pint / ⅔ cup full-
bodied red wine
300 ml / ½ pint / 1¼ cups beef stock
30 ml / 2 tbsp Marsala
10 ml / 2 tsp dried mixed herbs
salt and freshly ground
black pepper

Serves 8

1

Preheat the oven to 190°C / 375°F / Gas Mark 5. Season the meat well. Heat the olive oil in a large frying pan. When very hot, brown the meat on all sides. Place in a large roasting tin and cook for 1¼ hours.

2

Put the red peppers in the oven to roast for 20 minutes, if small ones are available, or 45 minutes if large ones are used.

3

Near the end of the meat's cooking time, prepare the gravy. Roughly chop the mushroom caps and stems.

4

Heat the frying pan again and add the pancetta or bacon. Cook until the fat runs freely from the meat. Add the flour and cook for a few minutes until browned.

5

Gradually stir in the red wine and the stock. Bring to the boil, stirring. Lower the heat and add the Marsala, herbs and seasoning.

6

Add the mushrooms to the pan and heat through. Remove the sirloin from the oven and leave to stand for 10 minutes before carving it. Serve with the roasted peppers and the hot gravy.

Bacon and Lentil Soup

Serve this hearty soup with chunks of warm, crusty bread.

INGREDIENTS

*450 g / 1 lb thick-sliced
bacon, cubed
1 onion, roughly chopped
1 small turnip, roughly chopped
1 celery stick, chopped
1 carrot, sliced
1 potato, peeled and
roughly chopped
75 g / 3 oz / ½ cup lentils
1 bouquet garni
freshly ground black pepper*

Serves 4

1

Heat a large pan and add the bacon. Cook for a few minutes, allowing the fat to run out.

2

Add all the vegetables and cook for 4 minutes.

3

Add the lentils, bouquet garni, seasoning and enough water to cover. Bring to the boil and simmer for 1 hour, or until the lentils are tender.

Creamy Layered Potatoes

Cook the potatoes on the hob first to help the dish to bake more quickly.

INGREDIENTS

*1.5 kg / 3–3½ lb large potatoes,
peeled and sliced
2 large onions, sliced
75 g / 3 oz / 6 tbsp unsalted butter
300 ml / ½ pint / 1¼ cups double
cream
salt and freshly ground
black pepper*

Serves 6

1

Preheat the oven to 200°C / 400°F /
Gas Mark 6. Blanch the sliced potatoes for 2
minutes, and drain well. Place the potatoes,
onions, butter and cream in a large pan,
stir well and cook for about 15 minutes.

2

Transfer to an ovenproof dish, season and
bake for 1 hour, until the potatoes are tender.

Traditional Beef Stew and Dumplings

This dish can cook in the oven while you go for a wintery walk to work up an appetite.

INGREDIENTS

25 g / 1 oz / 1 tbsp plain flour
1.2 kg / 2½ lb stewing steak,
cubed
30 ml / 2 tbsp olive oil
2 large onions, sliced
450 g / 1 lb carrots, sliced
300 ml / ½ pint / 1¼ cups
Guinness or dark beer
3 bay leaves
10 ml / 2 tsp brown sugar
3 fresh thyme sprigs
5 ml / 1 tsp cider vinegar
salt and freshly ground
black pepper

For the dumplings
115 g / 4 oz / ½ cup grated hard
white fat
225 g / 8 oz / 2 cups self-raising
flour
30 ml / 2 tbsp chopped mixed
fresh herbs
about 150 ml / ¼ pint / ⅔ cup
water

Serves 6

1

Preheat the oven to 160°C / 325°F /
Gas Mark 3. Season the flour and sprinkle
over the meat, tossing to coat.

2

Heat the oil in a large casserole and lightly
sauté the onions and carrots. Remove the
vegetables with a slotted spoon and
reserve them.

3

Brown the meat well in batches
in the casserole.

4

Return all the vegetables to the casserole and
add any leftover seasoned flour. Add the
Guinness or beer, bay leaves, sugar and
thyme. Bring the liquid to the boil and then
transfer to the oven. Leave the meat to cook
for 1 hour and 40 minutes, before making
the dumplings.

6

Form the dough into small balls with floured
hands. Add the cider vinegar to the meat and
spoon the dumplings on top. Cook for a
further 20 minutes, until the dumplings
have cooked through, and serve hot.

5

Mix the grated fat, flour and herbs together.
Add enough water to make a soft
sticky dough.

Country Pie

*A classic raised pie. It takes quite a long time to make,
but is a perfect winter treat.*

INGREDIENTS

*1 small duck
1 small chicken
350 g / 12 oz pork belly, minced
1 egg, lightly beaten
2 shallots, finely chopped
½ tsp ground cinnamon
½ tsp grated nutmeg
5 ml / 1 tsp Worcestershire sauce
finely grated rind of 1 lemon
½ tsp freshly ground black pepper
150 ml / ¼ pint / ⅔ cup red wine
175 g / 6 oz ham, cut into cubes
salt and freshly ground
black pepper*

*For the jelly
all the meat bones and trimmings
2 carrots
1 onion
2 celery sticks
15 ml / 1 tbsp red wine
1 bay leaf
1 whole clove
1 sachet of gelatine
(about 15 g / 1 oz)*

*For the pastry
225 g / 8 oz / 1 cup hard white fat
300 ml / ½ pint / 1¼ cups boiling
water
675 g / 1½ lb / 6 cups plain flour
1 egg, lightly beaten with a
pinch of salt*

Serves 12

1

Cut as much meat from the raw duck and
chicken as possible, removing the skin and
sinews. Cut the duck and chicken breasts
into cubes and set them aside.

2

Mix the rest of the duck and chicken meat
with the minced pork, egg, shallots, spices,
Worcestershire sauce, lemon rind and salt
and pepper. Add the red wine and leave for
about 15 minutes for the flavours to develop.

3

To make the jelly, place the meat bones and
trimmings, carrots, onion, celery, wine, bay
leaf and clove in a large pan and cover with
2.75 litres / 5 pints / 12½ cups of water.
Bring to the boil, skimming off any scum,
and simmer gently for 2½ hours.

4

To make the pastry, place the fat and water
in a pan and bring to the boil. Sieve the flour
and a pinch of salt into a bowl and pour on the
liquid. Mix with a wooden spoon, and,
when the dough is cool enough to handle,
knead it well and let it sit in a warm place,
covered with a cloth, for 20–30 minutes or
until you are ready to use it. Preheat the
oven to 200°C / 400°F / Gas Mark 6.

5

Grease a 25 cm / 10 in loose-based deep cake tin. Roll out about two-thirds of the pastry thinly enough to line the cake tin. Make sure there are no holes and allow enough pastry to leave a little hanging over the top. Fill the pie with a layer of half the minced-pork mixture; then top this with a layer of the cubed duck and chicken breast-meat and cubes of ham. Top with the remaining minced pork. Brush the overhanging edges of pastry with water and cover with the remaining rolled-out pastry. Seal the edges well. Make two large holes in the top and decorate with any pastry trimmings.

6

Bake the pie for 30 minutes. Brush the top with the egg and salt mixture. Turn down the oven to 180°C / 350°F / Gas Mark 4. After 30 minutes loosely cover the pie with foil to prevent the top getting too brown, and bake it for a further 1 hour.

7

Strain the stock after 2½ hours. Let it cool and remove the solidified layer of fat from the surface. Measure 600 ml / 1 pint / 2½ cups of stock. Heat it gently to just below boiling point and whisk the gelatine into it until no lumps are left. Add the remaining strained stock and leave to cool.

8

When the pie is cool, place a funnel through one of the holes and pour in as much of the stock as possible, letting it come up to the holes in the crust. Leave to set for at least 24 hours before slicing and serving.

Leek and Onion Tart

This unusual recipe isn't a normal tart with pastry, but an all-in-one savoury slice that is excellent served as an accompaniment to roast meat.

INGREDIENTS

50 g / 2 oz / 4 tbsp unsalted butter
350 g / 12 oz leeks, sliced thinly
225 g / 8 oz / 2 cups self-raising flour
115 g / 4 oz / ½ cup grated hard white fat
150 ml / ¼ pint / ⅔ cup water
salt and freshly ground black pepper

Serves 4

1

Preheat the oven to 200°C / 400°F / Gas Mark 6. Melt the butter in a pan and sauté the leeks until soft. Season well.

2

Mix the flour, fat and water together in a bowl to make a soft but sticky dough. Mix into the leek mixture in the pan. Place in a greased shallow ovenproof dish and bake for 30 minutes, or until brown and crispy. Serve sliced, as a vegetable accompaniment.

Orange Shortbread Fingers

These are a real tea-time treat. The fingers will keep in an airtight tin
for up to two weeks.

INGREDIENTS

115 g / 4 oz / ½ cup unsalted
butter, softened
50 g / 2 oz / 4 tbsp caster sugar,
plus a little extra
finely grated rind of 2 oranges
175 g / 6 oz / 1½ cups plain flour

Makes 18

1

Preheat the oven to 190°C / 375°F /
Gas Mark 5. Beat the butter and sugar
together until they are soft and creamy.
Beat in the orange rind.

2

Gradually add the flour and gently pull the
dough together to form a soft ball. Roll the
dough out on a lightly floured surface until
about 1 cm / ½ in thick. Cut it into fingers,
sprinkle over a little extra caster sugar,
prick with a fork and bake for about
20 minutes, or until the fingers are a
light golden colour.

Cranberry Muffins

A tea or breakfast dish that is not too sweet.

INGREDIENTS

350 g / 12 oz / 3 cups plain flour
15 ml / 1 tsp baking powder
pinch of salt
115 g / 4 oz / ½ cup caster sugar
2 eggs
150 ml / ¼ pint / ⅔ cup milk
50 ml / 2 fl oz / 4 tbsp corn oil
finely grated rind of 1 orange
150 g / 5 oz cranberries

Makes 12

1

Preheat the oven to 190°C / 375°F /
Gas Mark 5. Line 12 deep muffin tins with
paper cases. Mix the flour, baking powder,
salt and caster sugar together.

2

Lightly beat the eggs with the milk and oil.
Add them to the dry ingredients and blend
to make a smooth batter. Stir in the orange
rind and cranberries. Divide the mixture
between the muffin cases and bake for
25 minutes until risen and golden.
Leave to cool in the tins for a few minutes,
and serve warm or cold.

Scotch Pancakes

Serve these while still warm, with butter and jam.

INGREDIENTS

225 g / 8 oz / 2 cups self-raising
flour
50 g / 2 oz / 4 tbsp caster sugar
50 g / 2 oz / 4 tbsp butter, melted
1 egg
300 ml / ½ pint / 1¼ cups milk
15 g / ½ oz / 1 tbsp hard white fat

Makes 24

1

Mix the flour and sugar together. Add the
melted butter and egg with two-thirds of the
milk. Mix to a smooth batter – it should be
thin enough to find its own level.

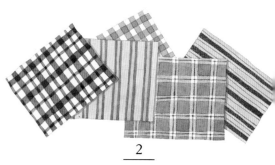

2

Heat a griddle or a heavy-based frying pan
and wipe it with a little hard white fat.
When hot, drop spoonfuls of the mixture
on to the hot griddle or pan. When bubbles
come to the surface of the pancakes, flip them
over to cook until golden on the other side.
Keep the pancakes warm wrapped in a tea
towel while cooking the rest of the mixture.

Christmas Pudding

The classic Christmas dessert. Wrap it in muslin and store it in an airtight container for up to a year for the flavours to develop.

INGREDIENTS

115 g / 4 oz / 1 cup plain flour
pinch of salt
5 ml / 1 tsp ground mixed spice
1/2 tsp ground cinnamon
1/4 tsp freshly grated nutmeg
225 g / 8 oz / 1 cup grated hard
white fat
1 dessert apple, grated
225 g / 8 oz / 2 cups fresh
white breadcrumbs
350 g / 12 oz / 1⅞ cups soft
brown sugar
50 g / 2 oz flaked almonds
225 g / 8 oz / 1½ cups seedless
raisins
225 g / 8 oz / 1½ cups currants
225 g / 8 oz / 1½ cups sultanas
115 g / 4 oz ready-to-eat
dried apricots
115 g / 4 oz / ¾ cup chopped
mixed peel
finely grated rind and juice
of 1 lemon
30 ml / 2 tbsp black treacle
3 eggs
300 ml / ½ pint / 1¼ cups milk
30 ml / 2 tbsp rum

Serves 8

1

Sieve the flour, salt and spices into
a large bowl.

2

Add the fat, apple and other dry ingredients,
including the grated lemon rind.

3

Heat the treacle until warm and runny
and pour into the dry ingredients.

4

Mix together the eggs, milk, rum
and lemon juice.

6

Spoon the mixture into two 1.2 litre /
2 pint / 5 cup basins. Overwrap the
puddings with pieces of greaseproof paper,
pleated to allow for expansion, and tie with
string. Steam the puddings in a steamer or
saucepan of boiling water. Each pudding
needs 10 hours' cooking and 3 hours'
reheating. Remember to keep the water level
topped up to keep the pans from boiling dry.
Serve decorated with holly.

5

Stir the liquid into the dry mixture.

Index

Aftershave, Dill 78
anchovies:
    Mediterranean Quiche 110
Apple Tart, French 140
Avocado and Pasta Salad with
    Coriander 114

baby:
    Baby Birth Gift 32
    Planted Basket for Baby 33
bacon:
    Bacon and Lentil Soup 146
    Griddled Trout with Bacon 107
Bag, Lavender 20
Baked Eggs with Double Cream
    and Chives 96
basil:
    Cod, Basil and Tomato with a
        Potato Thatch 108
    Spinach, Walnut and Gruyère
        Lasagne with Basil 135
Basket, Planted for Baby 33
bath:
    Bath Bags 62
    Bath-time Bottle 68
    Bath-time Treat Jar 68
    Herb Bath-bag 34–35
    Lavender and Marjoram Bath 80
    Lavender Bubble Bath 79
    Lemon Grass, Coriander and
        Clove Bath 80
Bean Salad, French 112
beef:
    Beef, Celeriac and Horseradish
        Pâté 128
    Roast Beef with Porcini and
        Roasted Sweet Peppers 144
    Traditional Beef Stew and
        Dumplings 148
Birth Keepsake 30
blackberries:
    Blackberry Charlotte 138
    Chicken Stew with Blackberries
        and Lemon Balm 130
Blueberries, Mackerel with
    Roasted 106
Bottle, Bath-time 68
Box, Shell 37
Bread, Wholemeal 99
Bubble Bath, Lavender 79

Cake, Lemon Drizzle 98
Calvados, Fish Stew with Parsley
    and Dill 89

candles:
    Shell Candle Centrepiece 38
cards:
    Greetings Card 27
    Patchwork Cards 24
    Pressed Herb Cards 66
Carrot and Coriander Soufflés 94
cases:
    Handkerchief Case 28
casseroles and stews:
    Chicken Stew with Blackberries
        and Lemon Balm 130
    Fish Stew with Calvados, Parsley
        and Dill 89
    Traditional Beef Stew and
        Dumplings 148
Celeriac and Horseradish Pâté,
    Beef 128
centrepieces:
    Herbal Tablepiece 58
    Shell Candle Centrepiece 38
chamomile:
    Bath Bags 62
    Chamomile and Honey Mask 70
    Chamomile Conditioning
        Rinse 76
Charlotte, Blackberry 138
cheese:
    Cheese Scones 136
    Leeks with Ham and Cheese
        Sauce 96
    Pear and Watercress Soup with
        Stilton Croûtons 105
    Spinach and Roquefort
        Pancakes 86
    Spinach, Walnut and Gruyère
        Lasagne with Basil 135
chicken:
    Chicken Stew with Blackberries
        and Lemon Balm 130
    Chicken with Sloe Gin and
        Juniper 132
    Country Pie 150–151
    Spinach, Cognac, Garlic and
        Chicken Pâté 128
    Spring Roasted Chicken with
        Fresh Herbs and Garlic 92
    Warm Chicken Salad with
        Sesame and Coriander 86
Chilli Gazpacho, Herb and 104
Chives, Baked Eggs with Double
    Cream and 96
Christmas:
    Christmas Pudding 156

Herbal Christmas Wreath 60
chutney:
    Pork and Mushrooms with Sage
        and Mango Chutney 130
Cinnamon and Orange Ring 54
Cleanser, Fennel 73
cloves:
    Lemon Grass, Coriander and
        Clove Bath 80
    Orange and Clove Pomander 55
    Rose and Clove Pomander 57
Cod, Basil and Tomato with a
    Potato Thatch 108
Cognac, Garlic, Spinach and
    Chicken Pâté 128
coriander:
    Avocado and Pasta Salad with
        Coriander 114
    Carrot and Coriander
        Soufflés 94
    Lemon Grass, Coriander and
        Clove Bath 80
    Stuffed Tomatoes with Wild
        Rice, Corn and Coriander 134
    Warm Chicken Salad with
        Sesame and Coriander 86
Corn and Coriander, Stuffed
    Tomatoes with Wild Rice 134
Corsages, Herb 63
Country Pie 150–151
Country Strawberry Fool 116
Crackers, Herb-decorated 65
Cranberry Muffins 154
Cream, Double, and Chives, Baked
    Eggs with 96
Creamy Layered Potatoes 147
Crumble, Rhubarb and
    Orange 100

dill:
    Dill Aftershave 78
    Fish Stew with Calvados, Parsley
        and Dill 89
    Smoked Salmon and Dill
        Pasta 114
dried flowers:
    Dried Flower Gift Wrap 46
    Dried Flowers as a Gift 47
    Dried Herbal Posy 61
    Dried Herbal Topiary Tree 59
duck:
    Country Pie 150–151
    Spicy Duck Breasts with Red
        Plums 133

Dumplings, Traditional Beef Stew
    and 148

Eggs, Baked, with Double Cream
    and Chives 96

Fennel Cleanser 73
Feverfew Complexion Milk 72
Filigree Leaf Wrap 42
fish:
    Cod, Basil and Tomato with a
        Potato Thatch 108
    Fish Stew with Calvados, Parsley
        and Dill 89
    Leek and Monkfish with Thyme
        Sauce 88
    Mackerel with Roasted
        Blueberries 106
    Smoked Salmon and Dill
        Pasta 114
Fool, Country Strawberry 116
French Apple Tart 140
French Bean Salad 112
fruit:
    Fruit and Foliage Gift-wraps 42
    Mixed Berry Tart 120

garlic:
    Spinach, Cognac, Garlic and
        Chicken Pâté 128
    Spring Roasted Chicken with
        Fresh Herbs and Garlic 92
Gazpacho, Herb and Chilli 104
Gift Tag 26
gifts:
    Baby Birth Gift 32
    Dried Flowers as a Gift 47
gift wraps:
    Dried Flower Gift Wrap 46
    Filigree Leaf Wrap 42
    Fruit and Foliage Gift-wraps 42
    Lavender Tissue Gift-wrap 44
    Tissue Rosette Gift-wrap 44
Greetings Card 27
Griddled Trout with Bacon 107

hair:
    Chamomile Conditioning
        Rinse 76
    Lemon Verbena Hair Rinse 74
    Parsley Hair Tonic 74
    Rosemary Hair Tonic 77
Ham and Cheese Sauce, Leeks
    with 96

Handkerchief Case 28
Heart, Scented Valentine 64
herbs (cosmetic):
    Bath Bags 62
    Chamomile Conditioning
        Rinse 76
    Herb Bath-bag 34–35
    Lavender and Marjoram
        Bath 80
    Lavender Bubble Bath 79
    Lemon Grass, Coriander and
        Clove Bath 80
    Lemon Verbena Hair Rinse 74
    Parsley Hair Tonic 74
    Rosemary Hair Tonic 77
    Tansy Skin Tonic 71
herbs (culinary):
    Baked Eggs with Double Cream
        and Chives 96
    Carrot and Coriander
        Soufflés 94
    Herb and Chilli Gazpacho 104
    Lemon and Rosemary Lamb
        Chops 92
    Mushroom and Parsley
        Soup 126
    Spring Roasted Chicken with
        Fresh Herbs and Garlic 92
    Thyme-roasted Onions 126
herbs (decorative):
    Dried Herbal Posy 61
    Dried Herbal Topiary Tree 59
    Herb Corsages 63
    Herb-decorated Crackers 65
    Herb Pot-mat 14
    Herbal Christmas Wreath 60
    Herbal Tablepiece 58
    Pressed Herb Cards 66
    Scented Pressed Herb Diary 66
Honey Mask, Chamomile and 70
Horseradish Pâté, Beef, Celeriac
    and 128

Ice Cream, Mint 118

Juniper, Chicken with Sloe Gin 132

Key Ring, Little House 22

Lacy Lavender Heart 18–19
lamb:
    Lamb and Leeks with Mint and
        Spring Onions 90
    Lamb with Mint and Lemon 109

Lemon and Rosemary Lamb
    Chops 92
Lasagne with Basil, Spinach,
    Walnut and Gruyère 135
lavender:
    Bath Bags 62
    Lavender and Marjoram Bath 80
    Lavender Bag 20
    Lavender Bubble Bath 79
    Lavender Sachets 16
    Lavender Tissue Gift-wrap 44
Leaf Wrap, Filigree 42
Leafy Pictures 48–49
leeks:
    Lamb and Leeks with Mint and
        Spring Onions 90
    Leek and Monkfish with Thyme
        Sauce 88
    Leek and Onion Tart 152
    Leeks with Ham and Cheese
        Sauce 96
lemon:
    Lamb with Mint and Lemon 109
    Lemon and Rosemary Lamb
        Chops 92
    Lemon Drizzle Cake 98
Lemon Balm, Chicken Stew with
    Blackberries and 130
Lemon Grass, Coriander and Clove
    Bath 80
Lemon Verbena Hair Rinse 74
Lentil Soup, Bacon and 146
Little House Key Ring 22

Mackerel with Roasted
    Blueberries 106
Mango Chutney, Pork and
    Mushrooms with Sage and 130
Marjoram Bath, Lavender and 80
Mask, Chamomile and Honey 70
Mediterranean Quiche 110
mint:
    Lamb and Leeks with Mint and
        Spring Onions 90
    Lamb with Mint and Lemon 109
    Mint Ice Cream 118
Mirror, Shell 40
Mixed Berry Tart 120
Monkfish with Thyme Sauce, Leek
    and 88
Muffins, Cranberry 154
mushrooms:
    Mushroom and Parsley Soup 126
    Pork and Mushrooms with Sage

and Mango Chutney 130
    Roast Beef with Porcini and
        Roasted Sweet Peppers 144
    Wild Mushroom Tart 124

New Potato Salad 112

Oatcakes 136
onions:
    Leek and Onion Tart 152
    Stuffed Parsleyed Onions 91
    Thyme-roasted Onions 126
oranges:
    Cinnamon and Orange Ring 54
    Orange and Clove Pomander 55
    Orange Shortbread Fingers 153
    Rhubarb and Orange
        Crumble 100

pancakes:
    Scotch Pancakes 154
    Spinach and Roquefort
        Pancakes 86
parsley:
    Fish Stew with Calvados, Parsley
        and Dill 89
    Mushroom and Parsley
        Soup 126
    Parsley Hair Tonic 74
    Stuffed Parsleyed Onions 91
pasta:
    Avocado and Pasta Salad with
        Coriander 114
    Smoked Salmon, Lemon and
        Dill Pasta 114
Patchwork Cards 24
pâté:
    Beef, Celeriac and Horseradish
        Pâté 128
    Spinach, Cognac, Garlic and
        Chicken Pâté 128
Pear and Watercress Soup with
    Stilton Croûtons 105
peppers:
    Mediterranean Quiche 110
    Roast Beef with Porcini and
        Roasted Sweet Peppers 144
Photo Frame 25
Pictures, Leafy 48–49
Planted Basket for Baby 33
Plums, Spicy Duck Breasts with
    Red 133
pomanders:
    Orange and Clove Pomander 55

Rose and Clove Pomander 57
    Spicy Pomander 50–51
    Tulip Pomander 52
Pork and Mushrooms with Sage
    and Mango Chutney 130
Posy, Dried Herbal 61
Pot, Shell 36
potatoes:
    Cod, Basil and Tomato with a
        Potato Thatch 108
    Creamy Layered Potatoes 147
    New Potato Salad 112
pressed herbs:
    Pressed Herb Cards 66
    Scented Pressed Herb
        Diary 66
puddings:
    Blackberry Charlotte 138
    Christmas Pudding 156
    Rhubarb and Orange
        Crumble 100

Quiche, Mediterranean 110

Red Tied Sheaf 56
Rhubarb and Orange
    Crumble 100
Rice, Wild, Corn and Coriander,
    Stuffed Tomatoes with 134
rings see wreaths and rings
Roast Beef with Porcini and
    Roasted Sweet Peppers 144
Rose and Clove Pomander 57
rosemary:
    Bath Bags 62
    Lemon and Rosemary Lamb
        Chops 92
    Rosemary Hair Tonic 77

Sage and Mango Chutney, Pork and
    Mushrooms with 130
salads:
    Avocado and Pasta Salad with
        Coriander 114
    French Bean Salad 112
    New Potato Salad 112
    Warm Chicken Salad with
        Sesame and Coriander 86
salmon:
    Smoked Salmon, Lemon and
        Dill Pasta 114
Scented Pressed Herb Diary 66
Scented Valentine Heart 64
Scones, Cheese 136

Scotch Pancakes 154

Sesame and Coriander, Warm
    Chicken Salad with 86

Sheaf, Red Tied 56

shells:

    Shell Box 37

    Shell Candle Centrepiece 38

    Shell Mirror 40

    Shell Pot 36

Shortbread Fingers, Orange 153

Skin Tonic, Tansy 71

Sloe Gin and Juniper, Chicken
    with 132

Smoked Salmon and Dill Pasta 114

Soufflés, Carrot and Coriander 94

soups:

    Bacon and Lentil Soup 146

    Herb and Chilli Gazpacho 104

    Mushroom and Parsley Soup 126

    Pear and Watercress Soup with
        Stilton Croûtons 105

Spicy Duck Breasts with Red
    Plums 133

Spicy Pomander 50–51

spinach:

    Spinach and Roquefort
        Pancakes 86

    Spinach, Cognac, Garlic and
        Chicken Pâté 128

    Spinach, Walnut and Gruyère
        Lasagne with Basil 135

Spring Onions, Lamb and Leeks
    with Mint and 90

Spring Roasted Chicken with Fresh
    Herbs and Garlic 92

Strawberry Fool, Country 116

Tablepiece, Herbal 58

Tag, Gift 26

Tansy Skin Tonic 71

tarts:

    French Apple Tart 140

Leek and Onion Tart 152

    Mixed Berry Tart 120

    Wild Mushroom Tart 124

thyme:

    Leek and Monkfish with Thyme
        Sauce 88

    Thyme-roasted Onions 126

Tissue Rosette Gift-wrap 44

tomatoes:

    Cod, Basil and Tomato with a
        Potato Thatch 108

    Mediterranean Quiche 110

    Stuffed Tomatoes with Wild
        Rice, Corn and Coriander 134

tonics:

    Parsley Hair Tonic 74

    Rosemary Hair Tonic 77

    Tansy Skin Tonic 71

Topiary Tree, Dried Herbal 59

Traditional Beef Stew and
    Dumplings 148

Treat Jar, Bath-time 68

Tree, Dried Herbal Topiary 59

Trout with Bacon, Griddled 107

Tulip Pomander 52

Valentine Heart, Scented 64

walnuts:

    Spinach and Roquefort
        Pancakes 86

    Spinach, Walnut and Gruyère
        Lasagne with Basil 135

Warm Chicken Salad with Sesame
    and Coriander 86

Watercress Soup, Pear and, with
    Stilton Croûtons 105

Wholemeal Bread 99

Wild Mushroom Tart 124

wreaths and rings:

    Cinnamon and Orange
        Ring 54

Acknowledgements

Appalachia: The Folk Art
Shop
14a George Street
St Albans
Herts AL3 4ER
(tel: 01727 836796;
fax: 01992 467560)
All things country

Brats
281 King's Road
London SW3 5EW
(tel: 0171 351 7674)
also at
624c Fulham Road
London SW6 5RS
(tel: 0171 731 6915)
Mediterranean palette paints

Farrow & Ball Ltd
Madens Trading Estate
Wimborne
Dorset BH21 7NL
(tel: 01202 876141;
fax: 01202 873793)
National Trust paints

Hill Farm Herbs
Park Walk
Brigstock
Northants NN14 3HH
(tel: 01536 373694;
fax: 01536 373246)
Suppliers of potted fresh
herbs, dried herbs and
flowers and dried flower
decorations

Manic Botanic
34 Juer Street
London SW11 4RF
(tel: 0171 978 4505)
Suppliers of made-to-order
floral decorations

Shaker Ltd
25 Harcourt Street
London W1H 1DT
also at
322 King's Road
London SW3 5UH
Mail order enquiries to
Harcourt Street address or
by telephone on 0171 742
7672
Shaker furniture and objects

Somerset House of Iron
779 Fulham Road
London SW6 5HR
(tel: 0171 371 0436)
Country furniture

Robert Young Antiques
68 Battersea Bridge Road
London SW11 3AG
(tel: 0171 228 7847)
Antique folk art furniture

The publishers would like to
thank the above mentioned
people for lending items for
photography.

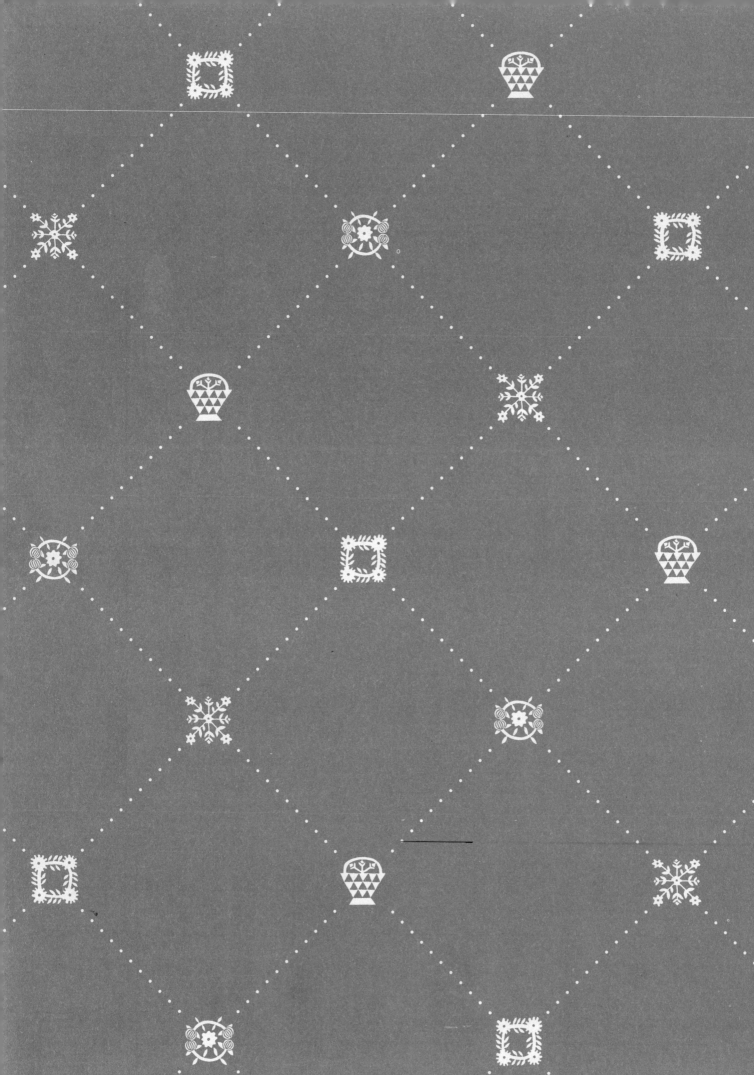